Falling in Love with Mystery

We Don't Have to Pretend Anymore

by

Richard F. Elliott, Jr.

DORRANCE PUBLISHING CO., INC.
PITTSBURGH, PENNSYLVANIA 15222

For information or to order additional books, please write:
Dorrance Publishing Co., Inc.
643 Smithfield Street
Pittsburgh, Pennsylvania 15222
U.S.A.

To Garnett

for Al,
with deep admiration,
respect, & devotion

PW

Acknowledgments

This book is indeed the work of the cosmos with countless human beings playing vital roles in its development. However, I wish to specifically thank a few people who were especially close to this process. Dick Daniels, Mark Conaway, Jean Childress and Mark Rouch reviewed my early manuscript and gave me very helpful feedback. They have also followed my progress and have encouraged me all along the way. My son James has been my computer consultant and has put the manuscript in decent form to submit for publishing. My wife Garnett has been unfailing in her loving support and patience. To these people I am forever grateful.

TABLE OF CONTENTS

CHAPTER ONE

HONEST TO GOD

It was during my eleventh year on the planet that it happened. I was walking through a pasture on our family farm and came upon a cow lying on the ground. It seemed strange to me that she would be lying so prone on the ground. I wondered if she were sick. However, it soon became apparent to me that she was in the process of giving birth to a calf. Until that time I was quite innocent about such things and was not convinced that calves were born in such a seemingly impossible way, but now all of that doubt vanished away. I was seeing with my own eyes a calf coming into the world. After a time of labor, the calf came gently out onto the green grass. It lay perfectly still for a moment and I wondered if it were dead. Then it took a deep breath and began to move. In a few moments the mother stood and began to lick her newest creation. Soon the calf was standing and nursing.

I was absolutely blown away! I was overwhelmed by awe. The mystery of life was as real and powerful in that moment as it has ever been for me. That is to say, I had a real life encounter with God. Then I returned to my normal religious training. Let me describe that.

I was born into a Pentecostal home. My mother's dad was a Pentecostal preacher. He died shortly after my birth, but Mother told me many stories of his ministry. They were amazing stories. On one occasion he spoke in tongues and a young man from Japan understood it as if Grandpa were preaching in Japanese. On another occasion a deaf man saw Grandpa speaking with sign language and understood everything he said although Grandpa knew no sign language at all. And one time Grandpa arrived to preach a series of services only to find that one of the most eager supporters of the revival had died. Grandpa prayed for him and the man came back to life. These were indeed amazing stories.

As I heard these stories, I was puzzled. My mother was not an unlearned person. She had attended college. She taught school for a few years. She ran a store and kept the books for a fairly large sawmill. Yet she told these incredible stories as if they were true. She believed them! I wondered about this matter. What was wrong?

Another thing I noticed. These stories did not disturb my mother's life. She told these amazing, impossible stories as if they were true and seemed to firmly believe them. At the same time she lived a perfectly normal life and raised her children and made sure they all went to college. None of her children even ended up in the Pentecostal church.

This was the first real quandary of my young life. What is this? A religion that takes for granted the truth of some utterly impossible stories and yet these beliefs seem to be disconnected from the rest of life.

Something else confused me. Not surprisingly, I began to wonder about the

1

Bible. There, too, are many impossible stories being told as absolutely true. The Christian people that I knew in my small circle all claimed to believe those stories. I knew these people to be solid, trustworthy citizens. Honesty was one of their central virtues. Yet they claimed to believe stories that were as far as I could tell impossible. And something else: It seemed to not make any difference in their living. They went on and lived quite normal lives. They had the arena of the stories and the impossibilities thereof thoroughly separated from their real living.

This was my earliest experience of the great separation which exists between religion and reality in our culture.

I entered college in the fifties. The county in which I grew up (Clarendon County, South Carolina) was embroiled in the very beginning of the civil rights revolution. I became involved in the Methodist Student Movement and in a short time was struggling very deeply with issues of justice. My entire life was having to be re-evaluated. By the time of my graduation, I was committed (in a white liberal way) to the cause of integration and racial equality.

I felt myself called into the ministry during my senior year in college. My "call" was impregnated with the issue of justice. I dreamed of preaching persuasive sermons which would move entire congregations of white people to change their segregationist ways. My hero was Amos. "Let justice roll down like waters..." (Amos 5:24 RSV).

Now I became aware of another confusing fact. The church was strongest in the southern United States and that was the very area where segregation had been most blatantly practiced. In fact, almost the only place on the planet where slavery lingered into the nineteenth century was the southern United States. What is this? A very strong religion is abroad in the land and a very great injustice is abroad in the same land. Where in the life of the white church could one hear a dissenting voice? Almost nowhere. The fabric of our country was stretched and torn. People died. Thousands were imprisoned. The church in which I grew up (the white protestant church in the South) was dragged kicking and screaming into the future. People I had known all my life, good honest church-going people, had no eyes with which to see the great issues of justice which were so crucial to the future of our nation.

This was my second encounter with the "great separation".

Shortly after I finished seminary I was back on the campus as a campus minister. This was in the mid-sixties. When I arrived on the campus I discovered that "everyone" was reading Bishop J.A.T. Robinson's book, *Honest to God.* That book marked the beginning of a new awareness in my life. Bishop Robinson had the courage to spell out clearly the problem that we face in the church: We live in a different world view from the world view in which our faith has been articulated for all these years.

A couple of years later I encountered Joseph Matthews and the Ecumenical Institute (Chicago). I attended a seminar called the Parish Leadership Colloquy. That event remains one of the formative events of my life. I was floating for weeks afterwards. The message I received was this: The Christian faith does in fact make sense in the twentieth century world! It is possible to articulate the ancient truths of the faith in language and thought-forms that make sense in our real world. I ended up spending seven years of my life on the staff/faculty of the Institute. We gave form to what was called the "Spirit Movement". The mission of that movement was to renew the church for the sake of a more just world. Those were very exciting albeit difficult years. Sometimes we would have fifty week-end seminars taking place across the United States at the same time. Lay people in the churches were concerned to see new life in the church. In the end, though, the movement passed by like one more fad. The church settled down to its old ways. *Honest to God* was forgotten. Joseph Matthews died and his battle-weary soldiers gradually turned to other interests. I returned to the local church and the work of being a pastor. There are few footprints left in the sand from the days of church renewal.

What is this? A religion that is mired in the world view and thought-forms of an ancient age and which seems unable to relate to the reality of its own time.

This was my third experience of the "great separation".

I encountered the Holy Mystery in the pasture. It was direct and personal. No reading was required and no rituals had to be performed. The Mystery had appeared to me...not in the supernatural, but in the *very* natural. And it was wonderful. It was life-transforming.

So what is this religion that seems so far removed from that close encounter with Mystery? What is this "Great Separation"?

In a way this separation comes quite naturally. We are born onto the planet. It is a mysterious planet in the midst of a mysterious universe. We are born without a clue. We know nothing. We have a few instincts and we have some involuntary activities that are already underway, but as to the actual situation of the planet and of the universe, we come aboard woefully ignorant.

There are, however, many "solutions" to the mystery close at hand. Others have been born before us with the same situation and they have tried to get a handle on things. They tell us that the earth is in fact round, that the water is dangerous, and that we should not play in the street. These things help. Later on, they begin to tell us more complex things...things having to do with life's more ultimate dimension. Life is awesome because there is a "God" somewhere who makes it that way. We should follow certain rules because God made those rules and handed them down to people in the distant past. You could say that we create an artificial universe to stand between us and the real universe which is so mysterious.

The unknown planet, not to mention the several hundred billion galaxies, is a bit scary for us all, so we are quite willing to accept the explanations that are handed to us. Recently a poll in the United States revealed that over half of the population believed that "Jesus will return". No one I have ever known could make much sense of that statement, but it has been handed down by supposedly wise people and well over half of us simply accept it. As an additional hedge against the impingement of the mystery, we have taught our children that such acceptance of hand-me-down dogma is a virtue. We have called such acceptance "faith"...a very puny usage of a very powerful word.

In an isolated culture the "hand-me-down" stories and explanations are easily accepted. But what happens when the entire planet becomes a village and the guy next door is a Hindu and the woman down the street is a Native American? What shall we do when the stories from all over are right here on main street? One would think that we would have a crisis on our hands. Not so. We go merrily on our way with the certainty that although there are other stories, the ones of our tradition are in fact the true ones. This requires a high degree of arrogance and/or intellectual inertia, but it does seem to be the order of the day. Yes, Jesus' disciple Peter did walk on water. And yes, the Buddha's disciple also did walk on water. The difference is simple. The story about Peter is true. The story about the Buddha's disciple is simply a story. That usually settles it. The point is that although our multi-ethnic society has given us an opportunity to gain some perspective on our hand-me-down religious stories and dogmas, we have not taken advantage of that opportunity.

One might also expect a change in science to make a difference in the religious stories and dogma. The science of the first century was radically different from the science of the twentieth century. The science of even the nineteenth century was very different from that of the twentieth century. Surely that would make a very great difference in our religious discourse. Not so. There are minor differences. The earth is discovered to be not the center of the universe and after a few centuries of denial, the church admits that sure enough the earth is not the center of the universe. Some still insist that the sun did stop for Joshua, but most of us suggest that perhaps the Bible simply means that the earth stopped turning for a while. More liberal folk suggest (quietly) that perhaps the story was speaking metaphorically. That is about as far as we have gone. An enormous change in our picture of the universe has made little discernable difference in the world view of our religion. We stand on tip-toe to receive the latest technological inventions of our day, but when it comes to our religion, we hold on, tenaciously, to the solutions of antiquity.

Thus we might describe the first of the two cornerstones of the "Great Separation" which denies our religion its rightful power. We, in our religious life, pretend that the world is as it was seen to be in the first century. We speak easily of a God who lives in heaven who sent his son down to earth. We tell the story of that son's trip back up to heaven and we assume that his primary residence is there...even until today. That story requires a universe which no longer exists, but our religion uses its language without apology or clarification. This pretension has created a chasm between our religious world and the real world.

The second cornerstone is this: We, in our religious preachings and teachings, pretend that our metaphors are facts. This robs the metaphors of their power and leads the hearers into illusion. The most blatant (though not the most serious) example is the Virgin Birth metaphor. As a metaphor, it has power. It is true that the birth that mattered in Jesus' life was not physical. It was not a matter of sexual

4

union. The Spirit was the source of his *real* birth. But if that metaphor is turned into a fact, it becomes self-defeating. It suggests that Jesus' spiritual power was related to his biological birth. It suggests that even God is somehow biological. It distorts the truth about God and about our own spiritual journey. Yet we will search in vain in main-stream church literature for a clear statement on the metaphorical nature of this beautiful story. Metaphors and symbols are the "surgeon's tools" of the spirit. They are used *because* literal words fail us in the deeps. Why would a people remove the most effective spiritual tools from the common life of the community?

These two illusions in tandem have rendered our religion incapable of spiritual power. They separate us from the situation of our living. The role of spirituality is actually quite the opposite. Spirituality is best defined as ***that dynamic in our lives which enables us to relate in a healthy fashion to the full reality of our situation***. A spirituality which encourages escape from reality is a contradiction in terms. Such a spirituality leads us to a shallow and dry existence in the midst of a universe of great depth and thirst-quenching refreshment. Shallow and dry people tend to seek help in all the wrong places. It is also true, and this is the most compelling reason for this book, that such people make poor workers in the struggle for a more just and healthy planet.

It is a natural tendency, as I said, to seek some comfortable way of relating to the unknown. It is even necessary. And, truth be known, all of our knowledge is penultimate. But what happens when our constructions no longer help us relate to the actual universe? What happens when they actually lead us away from the real and into a world of illusion and irrelevancy?

I contend that, for a long time, the universe itself has been calling us to a profound re-examination of our faith-story. Further, I contend that we have ignored the call. There has been a rather high price tag attached to our failure, but now there is a new dimension to the problem: The planet is in danger. The very survival of the planet's life-systems is imperilled. The mist of past illusions and denials is clearing away and the human community is seeing clearly for the first time the seriousness of the problem. Appropriately, almost every field of endeavor is turning its attention to the health of the garden in which we live and from which we gain our sustenance. The garden is dying. Given the same treatment it is presently receiving for a few more decades, life as we presently know it will be impossible. Now *that* is a new situation. It is a situation incomprehensible only a few years ago. I remember my dad telling me that a stream purified itself every few yards. The water filtered through the sand and purified itself. So also with rivers. The planet cleansed itself. Everything discarded by the road would rot and return to the soil. One did not have to be overly concerned. The planet took care of its own health. That was taken for granted. I don't know where Dad got that idea about the stream. It had been handed down for generations, I suppose. It made it easier to throw just about anything into the stream. But now, after just a few years, the story seems ludicrous. Our situation is radically different. We see the truth.

I say every field of endeavor is turning its attention to the problem. And so must those who are responsible for leadership in the realm of the spirit. The people who supposedly supply the most profound information concerning our relationship to our environment must now get to work. It is time for us to put our fears and our lethargy aside and work very diligently on the stories and dogmas which we teach and preach to the public. We must examine these matters afresh with this question uppermost in our minds: "What effect does this have on the health of the planet?" Especially the Christian community must come to terms with this issue because it is the Christian community that is leading the way in the trashing of the planet. Precisely the nations with the strongest Christian traditions are the nations that are doing the most damage to the environment. (Yes, the former Soviet Bloc countries were also bathed in the Christian story for centuries.) It is crucial now for us to look at our traditions and teachings with very open eyes.

Such a task will be mammoth indeed. We have neglected to adapt our religion to the changing times. We have not made the adjustments that need to be made. We have not updated. We have taken the easy way. Now the task is being thrust upon us by the universe itself. Our own survival is at stake. We must do the work of many generations in a fairly short time. The planet will not wait three hundred years for us to decide that "Yes, it is true that the earth is round". For instance, we had to struggle through the abolition of slavery with a Bible which was, on the surface, openly friendly to the practice of slavery. Lesson: We must help our people discern the difference between the "Word" which is timeless and the many "words" which are often tied to a very ancient time. But did that happen? Did we educate our people across the church that the Bible simply cannot be treated as a rule book which will give us specific guidance in every area of moral concern? Almost not at all. The discussions were held in seminary classrooms, but nowhere was it stressed that these matters must get into the pew! Bishops told jokes in sermons about young seminary graduates who tried to educate the laity in such "ivory tower" matters as textual criticism of the Bible. So today as we deal with the issue of homosexuality, we still have no distance from the hopelessly outdated biblical admonitions on the subject. Even more serious now is the Christian tradition's attitude toward the earth. As we seek to treat the earth more gently, we are finding very little support in our faith-story and that is indeed a matter of great urgency.

There is additional irony in this situation. Not only have we allowed our religion to become increasingly separated from the real world. Not only have we failed to learn the hard lessons of past moral struggles. We have lost a sense of what a profound spirituality can accomplish among a people. As Walter Wink has so ably helped us to see, the "real" spirituality of the United States informs us that we are a modern day incarnation of Matt Dillon or some other "man of steel". We believe in the redemptive power of violence. Things go badly, normal law enforcement is ineffective, and the hero comes in and solves the problem with violence. We tell ourselves this myth from the earliest days of childhood. As a result of that spirituality we were able to very easily gain a national consensus and go to war against Iraq. Can anyone imagine the story that we tell about Jesus having similar power in our nation's affairs? We have forgotten the importance of the spiritual dimension of life, and for that reason do not find ourselves alarmed. The religion of our time should not be expected to make much of a difference in our treatment of the earth or in matters of peace and justice. Why should it? When did it ever make much of a difference in issues of worldwide concern? We cannot remember a vital spirituality. We have forgotten its role in the human adventure.

My own experience on my own spiritual journey has convinced me that were we able to break free of the crippling illusions of our tradition, we would find a vital refreshing spirituality very close at hand. Very close indeed. I shall seek to describe that close-at-hand spirituality briefly here while saving a much more complete description for the latter part of this book.

Many, many years after my experience with the calf in the pasture, I hiked into the Grand Canyon. It was a glorious experience for me. And since that time I have had a love affair with the Canyon. Every two or three years I go back to the Canyon and hike its trails, sleep beside its streams, and bathe in its mystery. It is my holy place. It is my Mecca. It is where I touch the hem of "God's garment". Almost any place in the canyon I can pause and be brushed by the "wings of angels".

Certainly the Canyon is not the only place that affords such holiness, but for me it is the most reliable. The sea shore, the mountains, birds, spiders, little children and the Blue Ridge in the fall all tend to fill me with awe. It is spring as I write these words and just a day or two ago I looked at our river birch tree with its delicate fresh green leaves and thought: "Miracle!" Awe flowed through my blood stream.

You see, I am in love with mystery. Shamelessly, unabashedly, I am enamored with the mystery of life. I cannot get enough. I would walk a thousand miles, I think, just for the privilege of being blown away by mystery.

I find that the wonder of life is the spring from which the living waters flow. That is where I want to drink. That is the source of my vitality and my understanding of life. In fact, that is the source of my constant yearning for a more just world.

"Yes" is the word that I seek to have describe my life. I am delighted to be alive. I am endlessly grateful for the privilege of having shown up on the spaceship. The spaceship is in deep trouble and there is a terrific rebellion going on amongst the crew and the whole venture is in danger of extinction, but my love for the adventure is unabated. "Thank you" seems the most appropriate prayer, as Meister Eckhart suggested so long ago. Within my cosmic "yes" I also say my yes's and no's, but the "yes" is the description of my life and it is the style of living that I recommend to those who hear me preach.

Where does the "yes" come from? It comes from the mystery. It comes when I sit beside a stream in the Canyon and allow myself to receive the power of the mystery.

All of us are born into mystery. We come from mystery and we return to mystery. The truth of our existence is best stated simply that way: Life is utterly mysterious.

7

Moreover, I have discovered that such is the way it is supposed to be. It is so wonderful and life-giving to simply be in the arms of mystery that I could not possibly yearn for it to be otherwise. My yearning is only that I might be ever more aware of the mystery. My hope is that when I learn something on this planet, it will serve to increase my sense of mystery...my awareness of that which I do not and can't know or understand.

A few months before my dad died, I said to him that the older I got the less I knew. I said that I hoped that by the time I died I would know nothing at all. He laughed at that, but I was serious. For the truth is that all of life in its macrocosmic and microcosmic dimensions is utterly mysterious. Physicists tell us that it is not even certain that anything exists: It depends on who is observing and on when they are observing. Sometimes it is there. Sometimes it isn't. Sometimes it is a particle. Sometimes it is a wave. I want to be in touch with the universe as it really is. The way it really *is* is mysterious. Utterly mysterious.

The Bible tells us that one time Moses went up on a mountain and while he was there he had an encounter with God. Of course what actually happened was that he encountered mystery. He was awestruck. He had the same experience that I have at the canyon. His life was transformed! He saw what he had not seen before. He became energized as never before. His face had a strange glow when he returned to the folks below.

So it has always been. People are encountered by mystery. After that experience their lives are quite different. Sometimes their lives are different in a revolutionary way. Sometimes out of their experience and over some years a religion emerges. More likely they live out their lives in a full-of-life fashion and others see the aliveness and yearn for it and eventually construct a system to help other people live that way. Needless to say, that is a very tricky task. How do you give instructions about experiencing that which is utterly mysterious? Usually the danger is not avoided. Dogma is created which claims certainty for itself and very soon people are pledging allegiance to the dogma and are being shielded from the mystery. Certainly such is the case with Christianity in our time.

So, for my own purposes, I spell "Mystery" with a capital "M" (as I shall for the remainder of this book) and it is enough for me. I bend my knee there. I give my obedience there. I listen there. I learn there. I crawl on my knees up to the edge of Mystery and am not even aware of the blood on the path behind me. I am in love.

I think it is such love that makes the honesty for which I strive in this book possible.

I also think that it was this experience of being enraptured by Mystery which enabled our ancient ancestors to call it by the name of "Father". For them, I suspect, that was a gigantic and seemingly unavoidable leap of trust.

But suppose something happens in your life and you become distant from the Mystery. You become isolated from the springs from which the living waters flow. You no longer are being fed by the living bread. You are almost unaware of the glory, the majesty, the splendor, the Mystery of life itself. As Paul Tillich used to put it, you have become separated, alienated, estranged from the mystery, depth, and greatness of life itself. You are like a fish that has somehow landed on the dry land and cannot or will not find the water again. Your life has no zest anymore. Your source of oxygen is gone. You may still be flopping around on the beach, but for all practical purposes you are dead.

How can such a thing happen? The list is as varied as life itself. Perhaps you became enamored with yourself and imposed a kind of self-deception on yourself. You wanted life on your own terms and since "Mystery" is extremely uncontrollable, you distanced yourself from the awareness of Mystery. Perhaps you could not stand the pain that goes along with all real living, and you began to cut yourself off from pain. Perhaps you got tired of the nearness of death and tried to isolate yourself from death by accumulating material illusions of security. Perhaps you harbored serious uncertainties about life's significance and tried to cloud those uncertainties with drugs or work or shopping. The result is always painfully familiar: Deadness at the center.

The deadness itself is fairly easy to identify. All of life's joys tend to be artificial, such as constant watching of TV. Life's pain is held at a distance, such as the pain of 150,000 deaths in Iraq. One's own involvement in the suffering of the world is denied, such as any complicity in the plight of the homeless. The wonders of nature are no longer a source of nurture. One might go to the Grand Canyon and spend less than twenty minutes looking at what after all is only a "big hole in the ground". Then one might spend two hours in the gift shop purchasing mementos which might make it appear to the folks back home that one has been present to the wonder. One has to take pills to get through life's tragedies. At the funeral the most deeply bereaved person is in a drug-induced stupor. These and an infinite number of other symptoms signify the deadness. I understand that the Hindus have such symptoms catalogued and that the number runs into the thousands.

What hope is there for this condition? Is it hopeless? Left to our own devices it, at least in the abstract, would seem so. If we pull ourselves out of contact with the Source of life in order to build up our own illusionary world for the sake of a kind of artificial safety, why would we ever give up that fortress? In reality, however, we are more fortunate. Life does not leave us alone. The universe is so arranged that the misery of isolation can become overwhelming. Quite often before we breathe our last gasp of dry air, we flop ourselves back into the ocean. Or it might happen differently. The tide may come in and simply wash over us. The good news is this: Just as there are countless ways in which we get cut off from the fountain of life, so there are countless ways in which the Source of life reaches out to us and includes us in. My Papa died and that event dynamited some dams that I had constructed and the waters rushed in to compensate and to quench my deepest thirst. A young man goes to war and when he sees the first human being with a real face go down, he falls to his knees and sobs. From that moment on he is alive in a way in which he was never before alive. Another gets a diagnosis of cancer and suddenly avenues to the center are opened. Another simply looks out the window and sees a little bird in its pristine elegance and is instantly drawn into the vortex of Mystery.

Shug, in *The Color Purple*, described it beautifully. She said that during a time of deep despair she was suddenly reunited with the entire cosmos. She expressed the sense of unity in a phrase which I have remembered again and again: "I knew that if I cut a tree, my arm would bleed".[1]

Paul Tillich called this event "reunion". I think the Buddhists call it enlightenment. D.H. Lawrence called it "resurrection". In his wonderful poem "New Heaven and Earth" he describes it as vividly, I think, as ever it has been described:

....
God, but it is good to have died and been trodden out,
Trodden to nought in sour, dead earth,
Quite to nought,
Absolutely to nothing
Nothing
Nothing
Nothing

For when it is quite, quite nothing, then it is everything.
When I am trodden quite out, quite, quite out,
Every vestige gone, then I am here
Risen, and setting my foot on another world
Risen, accomplishing a resurrection
Risen, not born again, but risen, body the same as before,
New beyond knowledge of newness, alive beyond life,
Proud beyond inkling or furthest conception of pride,
Living where life was never yet dreamed of, nor hinted at,
Here, in the other world, still terrestrial
Myself, the same as before, yet unaccountably new.
......
Ha, I was a blaze leaping up!
I was a tiger bursting into sunlight.
I was greedy, I was mad for the unknown.
I, new-risen, resurrected, starved from the tomb,
Starved from a life of devouring always myself,
Now here was I, new-awakened, with my hand stretching out
And touching the unknown, the real unknown, the unknown unknown.[2]

---

[1] Alice Walker, *The Color Purple* (New York, 1982), p. 178.

[2] D. H. Lawrence, *Selected Poems* (New York, 1959), p. 75ff.

10

Jesus referred to it as being born afresh. The gospel metaphors abound: I was lame, but now I can walk. I was sick, but now I am well. I was possessed by demons, but have been set free. I was lost, but am now found. I was blind, but now can see. I was dead, but am now alive. My God, Yes! I am alive!

There is nothing especially "religious" about this event, in the way in which we normally think of "religious". This is just an event that happens in the midst of people's lives. It is just real life and it contains no "hocus pocus".

And so it is. Life is deeply and wondrously mysterious. We are enmeshed inescapably in that Mystery. The Mystery does not stop at Orion. It does not stop at the edge of earth's atmosphere. It does not stop at the skin surrounding my body. It is everywhere. Only when we are honestly and openly in touch with the "way it is" are we fully alive. We humans have the wonderful gift of "self-consciousness" which enables us to take a conscious stance toward reality. Sometimes in our weakness we take a life-denying stance. We build an illusion in which to live. That cuts us off from life and from its richness. But all is not lost: Life breaks down our protective devices and invites us to taste again the delights of the garden. When you stop to think about it, this is a pretty nice universe in which to live.

And something else: It seems to me, as I read the gospels, that Jesus was very often the occasion for this reunion. Perhaps for that reason people decided that he had a very close relationship with the Mystery: A relationship of trust such as a son might have with his father.

So we have this very strange situation: In the midst of a glorious universe where a very life-giving and life-serving relationship with Mystery is available, we have the "Great Separation" between our religion and that possibility. And that separation is not benign. It is, I believe, the major cause of our impotence in the face of enormous cultural challenges. I shall seek in the pages that follow to not only show in some detail the sickness that we have inherited, but to offer a more hopeful alternative.

CHAPTER TWO

THE REVOLUTIONS WE MISSED

I am not sure how conscious or un-conscious my dog is about the beauty she creates in the universe when she runs at full speed through the mountains. She surely is in touch with it at some level. However, I *am* sure that *I* am privileged to be aware of that holy creativity and I am privileged to self-consciously consider it and my place in it and make actual decisions about how it will flow through my own life. I, tiny little blip in a remote galaxy in the corner of the universe that I am, have the unimaginable privilege of consciously engaging myself in the creative process that has been going on across infinity for at least seventeen billion years. Oh, Mystery of the Universe, you have made me little lower than the angels!

Ah, but the glorious gift that I have just described can be missed. No, it is not possible to be excluded from the Holy Creativity of the universe. That creativity will flow through us in millions of ways no matter what. (It does the same in the case of the ant that just crawled across my notes.) But it is possible...yes, very, very possible to miss the glory of it. It is possible to miss the awareness of it. It is possible to not self-consciously participate in it. Perhaps a person is afraid of the deeps of life. That person will build barricades of illusion and distraction that will keep his/her awareness from sinking far enough into the earth to ever reach the mother lode. Perhaps one is so taken up with the accumulation of wealth that she/he is absolutely terrified of any awareness of the deeper concerns of the universe. Perhaps one was deeply scarred in early years and in defense has cut him/herself off from the wellsprings of life itself. Perhaps one has, most tragically of all, gotten into some religious system that seeks to describe the Holy Highway in language and thought-forms that are utterly unintelligible to a normal human being in the last decade of century twenty. Whatever the particularities, it is possible to miss it.

Well, I am determined not to miss it. I have my one chance to join the dance and I want to be awake for it. I want to allow the movement of the universe at its deepest levels of creativity to move me. I want to allow the deepest cry of the universe to touch me at the center. I want to venture, as King Arthur's knights were wont to do, into the forest at the darkest place where there are no pathways and where the only guidance I have is the guidance of the Mystery and my own heart. I want to use no excuses. I want to rely on no artificial answers. I want to accept nothing as true unless it vibrates as TRUE in the secrecy of my own center. I want to tell myself no lies! Absolutely no lies. I want to be in touch with the ceaseless flow of the Holy Creativity of the universe. I want to be caught in its currents and swim with it...even contribute to its movement and direction in my little way. And lo and behold, as I give my creativity to it, I am blessed to be able to see that the Holy Creativity of the Universe and my own creative efforts are one and the same. No, I don't feel deprived of "getting credit for my uniqueness". In fact, I feel overwhelmingly blessed.

Now it seems to me that the universe over these past half-dozen centuries has been working to make our existence even more blessed. If we can imagine that each new insight which helps us to see the way the universe really *is*, actually is a gift to us from the universe itself, then we can see that the universe is working pretty hard to make a more vital spirituality possible for us. Let me review a few centuries of that self-revelation.

The impact of the twentieth century penetrated the walls of Gethsemane Monastery in the early sixties and Thomas Merton wrote these words: "Our most important task is to become aware of the fact that our new consciousness of space no longer admits the traditional imagery by which we represent to ourselves our encounter with God".[3] Merton never followed that insight very far. Perhaps he would have, had he lived longer. He was just getting a hint of the glory of living without the great separation. It was being revealed all around him. But the story begins much earlier...back when Christianity was experiencing its birth-pangs.

The world in the first century was a two-storied affair. There was the bottom floor where we live our terrestrial lives and there was the top floor where we (hopefully) live our celestial lives. "There are celestial bodies and there are terrestrial bodies..." (I Corinthians 15:40 RSV). The bottom floor was seen to be flawed. Some used the word "fallen". It was a "vale of tears". It was, after all, only a poor imitation of the perfect world which existed on the second floor. Everyone knew about the first floor. They lived there. They experienced its trials and tribulations. Everyone also "knew" about the second floor. It was just above the spheres which held the stars in place.

In the western world where this two-storied picture was taken for granted, religions adapted themselves to it. What is the goal of every human being? Obviously, the goal is to get to the second story. Any religion that did not operate in this "real world" (as everyone saw it to be), would not survive. It is not clear that Jesus accepted this particular world view. It was, after all, a Hellenistic invention. It *is* clear, however, that when Christianity entered the Hellenistic world it had to face reality. Paul, it is generally assumed, did the majority of the theological work to get this feat accomplished. Jesus was transformed from a Jewish Messiah into a Universal Savior.

The second story was interpreted as synonymous with the biblical "Heaven". That is the place where God resides. Jesus came down to the first story to make it possible for us to get to the second story. Jesus has now returned to the second story and will live there throughout eternity. He lives there with his Father, who is God. Jesus came from the realm of perfection, therefore his life and his words were perfect. The entire story was tailored to the world-view of the time. That is what we

---

[3] Thomas Merton, *Conjectures of a Guilty Bystander* (Garden City, N.Y., 1966), p. 274.

have a right to expect of intelligent, responsible people: To live in the real world.

This somewhat strained marriage of the Jesus story and the first century world-view lived in relative peace for about fifteen hundred years. At that time a man named Nicolas Copernicus (1473-1543) came on the scene. Copernicus discerned that the old Ptolemaic picture of the universe was wrong. The earth was not in fact the center of the universe and was actually a small planet circling around a minor star in one galaxy of many.

It was not until Galileo Galilei (1564-1642), however, that the hypothesis of Copernicus was established as reliable science. From Galileo on, the old cosmology was gone. There was no second floor. There was no perfect realm separated from the imperfect realm. There was not even any "up" or any "down". The world was in fact a UNI-verse.

Here is a challenge for any religion. It is born in one world-view and for centuries tells its story in the confines of that vision of reality. As Thomas Merton stated it thirty years ago, Christendom "...conceived of itself as a world-denying society in the midst of the world. A pilgrim society on the way to another world."[4] Then the world-view changes. Can this religion still make sense if we change our story to fit the real world? What about our concept of God as the King sitting on the throne on the second floor? The throne room is gone. What might happen to the King? If there is no *place* for such a being, perhaps it is not possible to think of such a being existing. Perhaps one's entire way of speaking of the Mystery would have to change. Actually the response of the Christian church was to "kill the messenger", or at least to threaten him with his life. It was not until 1992 that the Vatican admitted the truth of Galileo's work...a long time indeed to wait for one's vindication. Meanwhile, the church chose to ignore the new cosmology. It decided to let science go its own way as long as it left the "religious" realm alone. Religion, meanwhile, would go its own way and pay no attention to any uncomfortable discoveries of science. It was a separation of religion from reality.

The damage caused by this arrangement has been enormous. The scientific community has been deprived of a conscience. Anything that is possible has been permitted. Today we see the results in unnecessary technology, dangerous chemicals, and atomic stockpiles. Meanwhile the religious realm has become more and more distant from the real world.

One could say that the Copernican revolution happened and the church missed it. The church's story, its rituals and its teachings are still wrapped in a pre-Copernican world view. We can only imagine what would have happened if the church had received the new cosmology as a glorious gift from God. Is it possible to imagine that even now we might change our story to fit the world in which we actually live?

Yet there was another revolution which we missed. To understand the enormity

---

[4] Thomas Merton, *Contemplation in a World of Action* (Garden City, N.Y.), p. 147.

of that revolution, we need to look briefly at the work of two men: Rene' Descartes and Isaac Newton.

Rene' Descartes is generally considered the founder of modern philosophy. He became convinced that it was possible to build a science that was based on absolute certainty. "All science is certain, evident knowledge. We reject all knowledge which is merely probable and judge that only those things should be believed which are perfectly known and about which there can be no doubts."[5] This belief in the possibility of "certainty" in the realm of science was to be the bedrock of Cartesian thought. We see now that he was wrong from this very early point. One can imagine that a vital Christian church could have revealed this to him at the time, but the church in its insecurity was holding on with white knuckles to its own "certainties".

Descartes is more famous for his statement: "I think, therefore I am". From this he went on to develop a system of thought that totally separated mind from body. That division has had a great effect on our civilization. While mind was venerated, all that was not mind was degraded. Matter was thoroughly devalued. There was no spiritual significance or possibility of illumination in matter. It was all mechanical. It could all, ultimately, be explained according to mechanical laws. One can see the philosophical framework being laid for an onslaught on the earth. Not only did the church not object, the church actually bought into this pattern of thought. The mind is the "real" part of us. The mind is more like God. The mind is the residence of the soul. God is Ultimate Mind. God is Ultimate Reason. We can get to know God through our own mental processes. Nature, meanwhile, is totally out of consideration as a locus of revelation. There is nothing sacred or mystical about nature. Such a view would be "pantheism". Nature is only a machine. Animals are only machines. The human body is only a machine.

Isaac Newton was born in 1642. He "...developed a complete mathematical formulation of the mechanistic view of nature, and thus accomplished a grand synthesis of the works of Copernicus and Kepler, Bacon, Galileo, and Descartes. Newtonian physics, the crowning achievement of seventeenth-century science, provided a consistent mathematical theory of the world that remained the solid foundation of scientific thought well into the twentieth century."[6] For Newton, space was absolute, time was absolute, and all matter was made of indestructible material particles. The entire world was a machine operating in space. God had created it all at some time in the past and it was functioning like a giant clock, governed by absolute laws. Again, the church found this view pleasing. The church, too, had her absolute laws. These too were formulated by God. It was comforting to have science support the idea of human certainty. Meanwhile spirit and matter were more separate than ever. Religions which still considered nature to be sacred were

---

[5] Fritjof Capra, The Turning Point (New York, 1983), p. 54.

[6] Ibid., p. 63.

15

considered primitive indeed. The stage is now set for the second revolution.

Albert Einstein (1879-1955) in the year 1905 published two articles which began a dual revolution in the way the cosmos is understood. "The two basic theories of modern physics have thus transcended the principal aspects of the Cartesian world view and of Newtonian physics. Quantum theory has shown that subatomic particles are not isolated grains of matter but are probability patterns, interconnections in an inseparable cosmic web that includes the human observer and her consciousness. Relativity theory has made the cosmic web come alive, so to speak, by revealing its intrinsically dynamic character; by showing that its activity is the very essence of its being. In modern physics, the image of the universe as a machine has been transcended by a view of it as one indivisible, dynamic whole whose parts are essentially interrelated and can be understood only as patterns of a cosmic process. At the subatomic level the interrelations and interactions between the parts of the whole are more fundamental than the parts themselves. There is motion but there are, ultimately, no moving objects; there is activity but there are no actors; there are no dancers, there is only the dance."[7] This revolution is staggering in its implications. Einstein himself was shaken by it, as he wrote in his autobiography: "All my attempts to adapt the theoretical foundation of physics to this [new type of] knowledge failed completely. It was as if the ground had been pulled out from under one, with no firm foundation to be seen anywhere, upon which one could have built."[8] Small wonder. In this new world the very thought process of the human brain seems to be pushed beyond its limits. Try to imagine this: In subatomic physics we find that matter does not definitely exist. It has tendencies to exist. Things don't happen in thoroughly predictable ways, but rather have tendencies to happen. Can nature be this thoroughly absurd?

Or to put it more to my liking, can nature be this mysterious? The Mystery has reappeared to the wondering eyes of the scientists. This must have come, after the initial shock of it, as very good news to Albert Einstein for he is quoted as having said, "The most important function of art and science is to awaken the religious feeling and keep it alive".[9] One might expect the church to celebrate the re-entry of Mystery (God) into the scientific arena. One would be disappointed.

So suddenly we live in a relative universe. Newton's basic building blocks are gone. Newton's absolute laws are gone.[*] Nothing is certain. There are probabilities,

<hr>

[7] Ibid., p. 63.

[8] P.A. Schilpp (ed.), *Albert Einstein: Philosopher-Scientist* (Chicago, 1970), p. 45.

[9] Matthew Fox, *Original Blessing* (Santa Fe, 1983), p. 66.

[*] It should be noted that Newtonian principles are still useful for penultimate purposes such as the design of automobile engines.

but not certainties. Newton's separation of the human mind from the rest of the cosmos is gone. Newtonian disdain for the natural world is now smothered in the realization that we are not separate from the natural world. We...including our brains...are natural, too. It is all one web of relationships. Modern physics is pointing us toward a unified and dynamic picture of the universe. Space and time are also dynamic and inter-related. They were both created at the moment of the cosmos' beginning. What was there before that initial creative moment? The human mind cannot grasp it. Sir Bernard Lovell put it this way: "There we reach a great barrier of thought because we begin to struggle with the concepts of time and space before they existed in terms of our everyday experience. I feel as though I've suddenly driven into a great fog barrier where the familiar world has disappeared."[10] One can only imagine the shock all of this has been for the self-confident devotees of the Newtonian model. Not to mention the church.

What, indeed, has the church done with this revolution? If the universe is uncertain and in a sense unknowable, does the church receive that as good news? Is this not a great opportunity for the church to offer its ancient counsel that "By trust we shall be saved". Not noticeably. The church has chosen to see this as another attack on its claim to certainty. Some in the church caught a glimpse of the ramifications of Einstein's theory and suggested that our moral laws were at best relative. The church leaders were outraged. "Situational ethics" was condemned from shore to shore. Is it not good news that the old mind/nature split is over? Can we not all rejoice that there is a possibility of having a healing relationship with the planet which has been so sorely wounded by the Newtonian era? Fritjof Capra has suggested that the healing possibilities are great for all of us since the old paradigm was so damaging: "...The Cartesian split between mind and body and the conceptual separation of individuals from their environment appear to be symptoms of a collective mental illness shared by most of Western culture, as they are indeed often perceived by other cultures."[11] Here is an opportunity to participate in the healing of these ancient wounds. Sadly, the church continues to live in the two-storied world of pre-Copernican days and continues to hold on to the spirit/nature split and the human certainties of Newtonian days.

It has been almost a century since Einstein published his articles. As of now, the church at large seems to have missed this revolution as well as the Copernican revolution. The shape of the first cornerstone of the great separation is getting clear. We are living in the illusion that two massive revolutions in humankind's very conception of the cosmos did not actually take place. We are choosing to reject the universe's offer of communion.

"Little Big Man" in the movie of that name became a gunfighter. He was taught

---

[10] Fritjof Capra, *The Tao of Physics* (New York, 1984), p. 183.

[11] Fritjof Capra, *The Turning Point* (New York, 1983), p. 368.

that in order to be successful he should learn to squint his eyes when he fired his six-guns. It turned out to be true. When he squinted, he was incomparable at his trade. Wouldn't it be something if we could "squint" and see the way the universe really is. We could see through everything. We could see the whirling electrons which make up the walls which surround us. There is in fact almost nothing solid in the universe, so we would walk gingerly across our lawns. One scientist is said to have worn snowshoes for a while after learning the truth about the nature of things. And something else: We could see the inter-relatedness of everything. Maybe we would see very thin webbing connecting everything to everything else. We would see a life line connecting us to the little girl in Managua who is selling her body and sniffing glue. And we would see an infinite number of lines connecting us to the countless galaxies and whirling planets. It would be a glorious picture. A cloud of awe would surely pass over us as it is said to have done on the Mount of Transfiguration. Love would flow out of us and through those spider-web connections as we sensed the inherent glory of all that is.

That possibility is given to us in our own time. It is a treasure beyond compare. It is also the avenue into salvation for our little blue planet. It is the way the universe cares for its own. To use older language: It is the way God cares for us.

Before we turn to a full consideration of that gift, let us more clearly delineate the contradictions of the great separation in the midst of which we continue to struggle.

CHAPTER THREE

OUR RELIGION: SEPARATED FROM REALITY

The Great Separation, as we have seen, has two dimensions. First, our religious discourse is conducted primarily in the language and images of the first century. It is as if going through the church doors takes us back to a cosmology that has been gone for a long, long time. It is rather difficult to imagine any excuse for such an incredible failure, but it is so pervasive among us that none of us gives much attention to it. The second dimension has to do with our metaphors. Our metaphors quite naturally are rooted in the cosmology of the era in which we pretend (in our religion and *only* in our religion) to live. However, the more serious damage is caused by our pretending that our metaphors are factual. The following pages give attention to the way this two-dimensional separation works itself out in our understanding of God, Jesus, Salvation, and Revelation.

GOD

Some ancient shaman in the very earliest days of our human journey had an incredible experience. One day s/he was able to turn loose the handholds and sink into Mystery. It was an overwhelming experience. The normal practicalities of life were set aside. The normal rational patterns of thought and belief were set aside. Sheer Mystery prevailed. It was similar to what we experience in dreams. In fact, I suppose dreams are the form in which Mystery touches us most easily and frequently, so it is not surprising that this shaman's experience should be akin to dreams. Wonder-full and awe-full images paraded through the consciousness of our early ancestor. Maybe there were images of eagles and bears and whales and wise old men and who knows what else. These images were of immense use to this shaman in the years that followed. They were used to help him/her in the task of relating to the Mystery of life.

In my life I have had two dreams which have been very helpful to me in relating to the Mystery:

In the first dream I was swimming in the ocean and was far from the shore. After a while I thought I should turn back toward the shore. When I did I saw a huge object in the water in front of me. After a moment I realized that it was a whale. Then suddenly there were whales all around me and I was quite frightened. Then I realized that I was privileged to be in a wonderful company of magnificent creatures. I determined to simply relax and appreciate the experience. I even thought: "This may kill me, but I do not have much control over it anyway and I want to receive the experience." So I gradually began to swim through the whales toward the shore. After a while I felt a pressure against the bottom of my foot. It was the head of a whale, gently pushing me toward the shore.

19

The second dream was similar. I was watching some bears in the mountains when suddenly one of the bears began to come toward me. I was frightened, but realized that running away was not likely to work out well. I simply stopped and allowed the bear to come to me. He made me stay with him, but did not hurt me. I was asleep beside the bear that night when a great fire broke out in the forest. The bear was up and seemed to be in the company of some other bears. I went over to him and put my arms around him and said, "I love you". He put his "arms" around me as well and held me in a warm embrace.

I have used bears and whales in my spiritual life ever since to remind me of the instruction of those two dreams. However, it would be quite erroneous for me to say that the Mystery is a bear or a whale.

Life is filled with a great and unfathomable Mystery. It is quite beyond our capacity to grasp. If such were not the case, we would not dignify it with the word "Mystery". Yet we must live in relationship to it. It is perhaps the most real thing in our existence. How did it happen that the exact genes came together so that you would be born? When and how is it that you will die? What is death like? Why are there so many different shapes of snowflakes? How do ducks eat grass and turn it into feathers? The whale and the bear came to me in the night to help me live in a healthy and life-giving relationship with that vast unknown. They suggested that I should put my life in the care of that Mystery and that by so doing I would live.

At some point in the past some shaman had a vision of the Mystery in the form of an old man. Perhaps it was during a time when a good and wise king ruled over the land and the vision took the form of a good and wise king, long gray hair flowing and seated on a throne. This vision was to inspire trust in the Mystery and help folks to be able to live a full life. The Mystery is like a wise and kind king.

Let us now get it clearly stated: The Mystery that is at the heart of the universe and which resides in every galaxy and in every atom and yet is to be equated with nothing that is; that Mystery is not a king seated on a throne any more than it is a whale swimming in the ocean. It is not a creature at all. It is at the center of all creation, but it is not a creature. It is not a being of any kind, not even a "supreme being". As Paul Tillich taught us, it would be better to use the phrase "Being Itself", though the truth is that no words can contain it. (No, not even the word "Mystery".) The Mystery transcends time and space and so is not located at any place, not even "Heaven". The Mystery is not a "Father". The image of "Father" should help us communicate the possibility of trust, provided that we have had some personal experience with a father worthy of trust. The Mystery, however, is not biological and therefore does not have offspring. Or, as one of our sister theologians in Brazil has put it, "This Mystery is what we call the Divine. But this Mystery is not a being, not a person. There is no God sitting on a throne who will judge us when we die."[12]

---

[12] Mary Judith Ress, "Ecofeminism and Panentheism," *Creation Spirituality* (November/December 1993), p. 11.

Why have we Christians chosen to single out one image for God and stay with that one image? We have even gone further: We have taught ourselves that the Father King on the Throne is actually the truth about God. We have not said that this is our choice of an image or symbol or metaphor for the Mystery. We have said that God really *is* a being who looks like a man and who had at least one child. "Have you talked to the man upstairs?" is not so far removed from the common mind of Christians. Why have we done this to ourselves?

Here the second dimension of the separation becomes visible. We are living in the illusion that our primary religious metaphors are factual. This illusion has combined itself with the one described in the preceding chapter. Together they have castrated the spirituality of the western world.

Certainly the disadvantages of such self-deception are readily evident:

It reduces God to a creature among creatures.

It is anthropocentric.

It makes God distant.

It promotes patriarchal behavior among us.

It neglects non-human creatures.

The greatest disadvantage of all, though, we usually miss: This old image of the "King" on the throne in heaven is from a picture of the universe that no longer exists. As we have seen, in the first century there was (according to the science of the day) an upper level in the universe. There was the earth down here and there was up above us another realm. That upper realm was in fact the more real one. Down here was just a temporary home. If a person could get ahold of the right knowledge (so the gnostics taught), s/he could leave this second-rate place and go upstairs to the first-rate place. That first century view of the universe was never very comfortable for the Hebrew people and Christianity fit into it with considerable difficulty, but now we can let that struggle go. That universe is gone. There is no upstairs and downstairs. We live in a UNI-verse.

WE LIVE IN A POST-COPERNICAN, POST-EINSTEINIAN WORLD AND WE HAVE OUR RELIGION STILL BEING ARTICULATED IN SYMBOLS AND THOUGHT FORMS OF A PRE-COPERNICAN, PRE-EINSTEINIAN WORLD. TO COMPOUND THE PROBLEM, WE HAVE TAKEN OUR PRE-COPERNICAN METAPHORS AND DECLARED THEM TO BE ABSOLUTE FACT.

But what about our great emphasis on a "personal" relationship with God? How can one have a personal relationship with a God that is not in some sense a "being"? I remember the objections to Paul Tillich's "Ground of Being". "How can you have a personal relationship with a 'Ground of Being'?" This super-concern for the word "personal" in our religious conversation has always puzzled me. When I have experienced the Mysterious Center most vividly there has been no sense of my

21

encounter being with a "person" of some kind. Yet, at the same time, those experiences were always very personal for me. They were life-changing for me as a person. When I stood by my father's open grave and shoveled the earth onto his coffin, I was overwhelmed by a sense of awe-full wonder. It certainly was a very personal experience of Mystery, but there was no sense of the Mystery being some kind of a "person". In fact, I usually find that the word "God" gets in my way. It reduces the Mystery down to a creature that can be called by a name. It carries all the old baggage of a world view that is no longer my own. I also find that personal pronouns are not helpful. Calling the Final Mystery of the universe "He" or "She" seems almost ludicrous to me. I use the language in my church, but I use it with discomfort.

The truth, of course, is this: We use personal language for God in an effort to control God. If we can get God into some kind of a human image with a human shape and a human brain and human emotions, then we can put some limits on that which can't be limited, a perpetual temptation for us humans.

Notice the libraries of books that have been written in an effort to explain why God behaves the way God does. They assume that God should pretty much abide by our human rules and codes of conduct. Why does God cause cancer? Well, we all agree that no loving Father could ever cause cancer, so our human logic tells us that God is not involved in cancer. Oops! Suddenly we have separated the Mystery that pervades every atom in this universe from those atoms that are involved in cancer cases. God is now smaller. More human-like, but smaller. Take the issue of tidal waves. Why does God cause tidal waves to drown thousands of people? Oh my goodness, of course God does not cause tidal waves. They just happen. It is just nature. God does not even intend that they happen. Now our God is not even in charge of nature. What *is* this God in charge of?

The uncomfortable truth is that the ways of the Mystery are (of course) mysterious. We cannot understand them. Sometimes they are simply horrible. What shall we do? Go to another universe to live? Write libraries trying to justify our God's behavior? Pretend that we understand what those very libraries by their existence testify that we don't understand?

Furthermore, to make God in the image of a man makes the whole matter more difficult. Since it is clear from moment one that the way this universe operates is not according to any human sense of right and wrong (incredible suffering, innocent deaths, natural catastrophes) it would seem extremely unhelpful to posit a God who acts and thinks like a human. Why not simply trust? Why not simply trust? Consider Job. Awful catastrophes come along. There is no rational explanation. These things happen to some extent in everyone's life. Shall we confuse ourselves like Job and his friends illustrate so well for us? Or shall we simply trust, not knowing, as Job finally was persuaded to do?

Here is my recommendation: Experience in the real world the awesome Mystery that is at the center of life no matter where you show up. Decide in fear and trembling to relate your life to that Mystery. Fall in love with it. See the wonders and the catastrophes that flow mysteriously from the Center of life. Sometimes in delight, sometimes in fear and trembling decide to trust that great Mystery. Not because it is your first choice, but because as far as you can see it is your only choice if you are to live in the real world with your integrity intact. In that trusting, you discover that life is filled full and you dance around the campfire. You celebrate existence itself. You celebrate your own chance to be present.

Here is the other option: Experience in the real world the awesome Mystery that is at the center of life no matter where you show up. Notice the unpredictable and uncontrollable nature of that Mystery. Give that Mystery a name and set out to domesticate it. Set out to control it. Begin to fabricate characteristics which "He" or "She" must have. Give it a place to live that makes sense in your world view or failing in that in some ancient world view. Write philosophies and "systematic theologies" about it. Seek to know that which is unknowable. Accept the idea that in the distant past that Mystery revealed itself to some great saints and that those saints wrote it all down in a book. If you are especially insecure, you can posit that the book is incapable of error. Then, lest someone raise a question, proclaim that the greatest good in the world is the acceptance of the whole system without question. Call that "faith". In fact, you might persuade yourself to believe that one's life will be extended for all eternity as a result of accepting the entire package without the slightest doubt.

Such an option as this second one can survive a long time. We humans love to believe comfortable things about that which is actually pretty unsettling. We enjoy having easy answers to difficult questions. Illusion is a mighty temptation in all ages. However, when the world view of the illusion disappears, the cracks in the facade become more evident. We live in such a time. And when the times are extremely critical and are demanding a revolution in the depths of the human spirit, it is especially unfortunate to be saddled with a religion which refuses to come to terms with the real world.

JESUS

Try to imagine this: Long, long ago in a distant country a man owned a huge manufacturing plant. He had built the plant from nothing. He was the sole owner. He had many employees. After a period of time the employees came to have a rebellious attitude. Perhaps they thought they should get their way a bit more often. In any event, relations became strained. The owner of the plant finally reached a desperate place. He was at his wit's end. One day he had a great illumination: "I will take my little girl, my only child, and cause her to die a horrible death. I will then tell the workers that I gave her up so that they would come back into a harmonious relationship with me." Note that the owner is not sacrificing his own life for the sake of an improved relationship. He is sacrificing his innocent child.

One can imagine that in biblical days this story was acceptable. People were familiar with a great variety of sacrificial systems which were supposed to improve the divine-human relationship. It was also true in those days that children were often considered the property of their parents and parents could dispose of them as they wished. See Genesis 19:8 for a graphic illustration. Lot would sacrifice both his daughters for the sake of a couple of strangers who happened to be his guests.

Today, though, that story simply won't do. Quite obviously, the problem belongs to the father. Why bring the innocent daughter into it? And why can't the father solve this issue with his own resources. And no parent has a right to sacrifice his or her child to solve a problem. No way!

Yet we unabashedly continue to tell such a story at the very center of our religion. What kind of a God is that? A powerless God who must depend on his child's blood to solve relational problems? The old Calvinist Catechism put the matter most bluntly, "He, all the time of His life, but especially at the end thereof had borne in body and soul the wrath of God against the whole human race." And for people who are no longer schooled in the old sacrificial systems the next question is obvious: How is that going to help the relationship anyway? To go back to our original story, are the workers going to be impressed by the action of the owner in having his own child killed? They would feel some pity, but as soon as the funeral was over they would say, "Well, what about the issues we were discussing before this horrible thing happened?"

Give us credit: We have labored hard and with incredible twists of logic to make sense of that story. The devil was in charge of the workers and demanded a child-sacrifice in order to release them from his control. There was no hope that the workers would turn from their evil ways except the most supreme sacrifice be made. All these efforts test human credulity.

So here is our dilemma: We have a story at the center of our religion that in our world is extremely irrational. God is a being who can actually have a son. God sent his son to earth to die for the sins of all humankind. The son was killed, was buried, and then came back to life. After a time of appearances and disappearances this son returned to the throne beside the father in heaven and lives there even as we speak. But, in fact, God is not a being at all. God is not only not a biological being, God is not any kind of a being. God did not have a "son". And the two of them do not live in a place called heaven.

The biblical story is actually better in this case than our current understanding and language. The gospels are comfortably confusing enough to give the clue that our mamas and papas of the faith knew that they were speaking poetically or metaphorically. Luke and Matthew invent birth narratives to fit their own theological intentions: Luke to emphasize the value of the "least of these", Matthew to emphasize the majesty and universality of the event. If such incredible events had been literal we can be sure that Paul and Mark and John would have felt constrained to mention them. Of course they were not literal. A recent newspaper article seriously questioned how many babies it was likely that Herod killed. No babies were killed! That was just part of Matthew's plan to get Jesus into Galilee where everyone knew Jesus actually lived. And of course Matthew used his very strained method of Old Testament proof-texting to indicate that the prophets predicted a trip to Egypt for Jesus. No matter. It is all story. It is not something that actually happened. It seems fairly clear that the biblical authors rested easily with symbol. In our day we do not.

I believe it was that comfortableness with the metaphorical that enabled the story to catch on and carry with it the creation of a world religion. Nonetheless, one does not have to look very hard to discover a considerable amount of strained logic in our church history. Listen to the explanations of the Trinity. Listen to how it is that Jesus is very man and very God. Metaphorically speaking, one might handle it. Literally speaking, it defies logic. But give us credit. Our very best thinkers dedicated years of blood, sweat and tears to these issues.

Now we come to the question: In the midst of this enormously complicated body of handed down interpretation, what is the "pearl of great price?" What is the deep truth that we might preserve from this story that might be helpful to every human being on the earth were we able to transfer it into our own world-view?

We could tell the story this way: Once there was a man named Jesus. He was an extraordinary man. He embodied love for humankind as well as love for the Mystery. In fact, when we looked at him, it seemed that we "saw through" to the way life could be lived in a very full and abundant way. Because of this world's discomfort with the transparency of the man, he was executed. Those who were close to him in life were deeply moved by his death. They experienced a unity with him and with his way of living that went beyond the grave. It could be said that in him the Mystery of life was laid bare. It could be said that in an incredible way, he was "at one" with the Mystery itself. He trusted it, and enabled others to have that trust. Those who placed their trust there found their lives filled full. They had life and had it abundantly.

Get acquainted with him as much as is possible over two thousand years of time and through considerable accumulated confusion. Try to let the spirit of living that was in him, be in you. Learn to trust the Mystery and love the creation as he did. Is that enough? Is it really any help at all to accept the early church's interpretation of his death? It was helpful in their cosmos, but it is not in ours. It is also worth mentioning that if we confine ourselves to the undisputed words of Jesus in the New Testament, we find no suggestion that Jesus saw himself as the universal solution for sin. Rather the sin he seemed most interested in was the hypocrisy of religious leaders who cared more for their system than they cared for people.

I believe the bare bones reason for the Jesus story is that it gives us confidence in the Mystery. Life is very confusing, frightening, and absolutely uncertain. Jesus is a picture of a man living victoriously in the midst of that vast uncertainty. Life is a sea of tumultuous waves and deep dilemmas. Jesus was seen walking confidently across that sea. Trust! Trust! As Dietrich Bonhoeffer taught us, Jesus' divinity is to be found in the completeness of his humanity. Trust that picture of full humanity. Of course, that story would not be of much help if we ourselves did not now and then validate it in our own lives. The story takes on power for us only insofar as we

25

now and then are able to trust that life is at the Center trustworthy and accordingly find life profoundly altered in its quality. (Sometimes that experience is so powerful that we might refer to it as a "second birth".) So in that sense, Jesus is really me. Jesus is really you. We recognize him for that reason.

And I find myself excited about that story. It is a story I could tell my grandchildren. But please don't tell me I have to include the language about "up in heaven" and "Jesus dying for my sins" and "a body actually coming out of a grave". That doesn't help. Instead, that turns it into an extremely confusing relic out of a bygone age. Such confusion does not however stop us from continuing to claim that our Jesus is the only solution to every human being's deepest spiritual need.

A few months ago our United Methodist magazine for clergy devoted an issue to the question: Is Jesus the only way to salvation? It is the late twentieth century and that ancient question is still being asked and serious debate is going on about it.

One is reminded of the old question: "If a child were born in deepest Africa (Why did we always use Africa for this question?) and never got a chance to hear about Jesus and then died...would that child go to heaven?" This was always a very difficult question for the more insecure Christians. If that child could in fact go to heaven, that would raise serious questions about our missionary enterprise and even about the importance of our own conversion. If that child went to hell, that would raise serious questions about the goodness of our God.

Or what about the very devout Buddhist who followed very diligently the very best that he knew? Is he going to have to burn in hell forever just because he made the mistake of being born into a Buddhist culture?

The entire discussion, however, betrays a failure to enter the twentieth century. The discussion depends on a first century world view where heaven and hell are places to which one goes for eternity and where God is a being of some kind who sits on a throne and makes heaven or hell decisions for folks as they die. This world view had a certain built-in disadvantage. You either entered the second story or you didn't. There was not much room for life's normal ambiguity. We tried to introduce purgatory to gentle the stark dualism, but it was a poor solution. Probably the radical dualism of Zoroastrianism was to blame for much of that problem. How tempting to reduce all of life's ambiguities down to two eternal options. No matter. That universe has long since departed our company. Accordingly, let's leave that world behind and have the discussion in the twentieth century.

The Mystery is in the midst of life. Every human being is immersed in it. Our relationship to the Mystery is similar to the relationship of a sponge to the sea. The sponge is thoroughly in the sea and the sea is thoroughly in the sponge. The Mystery is totally in us and we are totally in the Mystery. The question is whether we will relate to it in a life-giving way or not. Many people in all parts of the earth do in fact reach out and put their arms around the Mystery and hold it to themselves in glorious devotion. They have received salvation. They have the experience of contact with the eternal. Many others do not. For reasons we have already discussed, they decide to live in illusion. They prefer darkness to light. So on a given day, there are many people who have received salvation and there are many who have not. Many are experiencing "eternal life" (life which is related to that which is eternal) and many are not. What happens when these people die, we know not. We have various metaphors from antiquity, but they are not much help in our present world view. They are more thoroughly impotent because of our tendency to treat them as literal descriptions. We have no metaphors that are rooted in our own time. That is one way of describing our present spiritual poverty.

In a discussion such as this, it helps to consult one's own experience. How is my relationship to the Mystery? Do I experience it as a very fixed thing? Something that I might basically settle at the age of puberty? Can I by a decision early in my life assure that for my remaining years I will live in a relationship of trust with the Mystery? Is salvation really a matter that is ever clearly settled? In actuality I can be deeply in love with Life (spelled with a capital "L") and then have some painful experience come along and wreck the train. Maybe for days I will have to struggle to remember again the glory of being alive. Isn't that actually the way life is? No matter that we wish it otherwise. Of course we do. Of course we long to have the ambiguity of life removed. How tempting to believe that I could "make a decision for Christ" and have my entire life made secure...here on earth and for all of eternity as well. How tempting to condemn everyone who has made a decision different from mine to eternal damnation. This one factor in our traditional faith screams out the word "INSECURE!" for all the world to hear. Let that all rest now. The universe we live in is very dynamic and uncontrollable. Life is all mysterious. Our own relationship with the Mystery is included.

What has Jesus to do with this scenario? Better to ask the question this way: "What has Christ to do with this?" Christ is a name we might reasonably use for the eternal quality in this universe which enables us, without three good reasons, to trust the Mystery. That "Cosmic Christ" is everywhere present. It was present in Jesus to a remarkable degree, but it is not limited to him. "In the beginning was the Word (read Cosmic Christ) and the Cosmic Christ was with God and the Cosmic Christ was God."(John 1:1) So, we can say, anywhere a human being trusts the Mysterious Center, there the Christ is present. If one is wedded to the old dogma, one could continue to say, "There is no salvation outside of Christ". But, of course, loose use of such a phrase without translation identifies one as a dinosaur.

This is understandably frightening to the institutional Church. By implication all religions might have "Christ" right in their midst, albeit not by that name. Of course they do! To the extent that any human being in that religion is living in "communion" with the Mystery, Christ is present. To the extent that any human being in that tradition has said a glorious YES to life in all its depth and glory, Christ is present. Christ is the quality that makes such trust possible. Fortunately, the Christian branch of religion does not control where Christ might show up.

The test of a religion, then, might not be whether it uses the language of the Christian faith and follows Christian dogma, but whether it is helpful to Christ;

27

whether it moves people toward trust in and unity with the Mystery. I am not well acquainted with other religions, but my suspicion is that all major religions on this planet are in a situation similar to that of Christianity. Those religions are likely mired in ancient world views and thought-forms. Their leaders have probably been frightened by the changing times and have been tempted to treat the legends and myths of their tradition as historical facts. Therefore, their religion is quite likely leading people into illusion rather than into joyful union with reality. However that may be, if a person is constantly falling in love with the creation and its mysterious Center then that person is enjoying what has traditionally been called salvation...Communion with God.

Yet, amazing as it may sound, these very days mail is crossing my desk from various splinter groups in United Methodism stressing the importance of a return to a strong emphasis on Jesus as the only way to salvation. The gradual weakening of our denomination, they say, is due to our failure to hold onto the solid doctrines of the past. Actually, the truth is quite the opposite.

SALVATION

Imagine our ancient shaman friend. S/He was the first human being to actually, in a self-conscious way, be aware of the Mystery. S/He was struck by awe and felt a deep sense of unity with the entire creation and its Mystery. Our friend was blessed, blissed, and in a profound way, healed. S/He felt a wonderful sense of gratitude for being alive and for being a part of such a glorious enterprise. At that moment s/he was so deeply "in love" with the cosmos that not one thing in it was unimportant. It was all holy.

It did not occur to this ancient human being to want something more. It was all so overwhelmingly glorious, how could one possibly wish for more? Oh, one might wish that the fruit would fall off the trees at one's bidding, but such a desire seemed extremely unimportant in the midst of such ecstasy. And, as a matter of fact, it probably seemed to this shaman that the struggles of life were part of the gift. It was all shrouded in holiness.

That, in my view, is what salvation is. That shaman experienced salvation. Salvation is the experience of unity with the central Mystery of life. When one has such an experience of unity, the fullness of it is simply overwhelming. My heart is restless until it returns to that sense of unity.

Now get ready for a giant leap:

We do not like life on this planet, so we posit a better place to go when we die.

We do not like the limitations of time that are part and parcel of our real living, so we posit a place that is timeless.

We do not like the suffering and dying that are central to full living on this planet, so we posit a place where there is no suffering and dying.

We don't like living under financial restraints, so we posit a place where the very streets are paved with gold.

As a matter of fact, we don't like any hardships at all in life and so we posit a place where there are none.

We can't stand seeing some people profit from evil and so we posit a place where all injustices are evened out.

We can't imagine forgiving people who don't apologize to us, so we posit a place of eternal torment for people who don't apologize to God before they die.

What must we make of all this? As we have seen, it certainly pre-supposes a cosmology that no longer exists. But regardless of cosmology and regardless of Plato's teachings there is this: We do not like the real world as it has been given to us and so we decide that there must be a better world somewhere else. One could also argue that it is our effort to make sense of the problem of human suffering. Why do some people who are so good have to suffer so much? Reincarnation is the vehicle of solution for the Hindus. Heaven and hell are the Christian solution. Regardless of the excuses we might offer, we are left with a very other-worldly, escapist view of salvation. Salvation is to go to heaven when you die. This life is a vale of tears and if we behave appropriately we will get to go to a really good place when we die. Certainly we have made this a bit more sophisticated in our time. We don't "dangle people over hell" like we once did. We don't speak in quite such crass terms as we once did. But the truth remains that Christianity has been infected with this "escapist" virus for a long time.

Actually, in the more "liberal" or "mainline" churches, the escapism is more subtle. We don't speak of "going to heaven" very much. Normally we only mention that at funerals and at Easter. More likely our sermons will speak in vague terms of being "committed to Christ". Most of the time the "committed to Christ" is touched lightly and the sermon goes on to speak about how that works out in terms of being willing to teach Sunday school classes when asked and being willing to support the church financially. In really progressive churches there might be some mention of contemporary social issues. Quite often various issues of normal family life are also mentioned. Remove the vague reference to being committed to Christ and a few biblical references and the sermon could be an after dinner speech at the local service club. So where is the escapism? It is in the vagueness of the reference to Christ (or to God as the case may be). Remember this is *not* the local service club. This is the place where the Ultimate is supposed to be honored. Yet when people arrive they are invited to commit themselves to a Christ who is extremely abstract. What does it actually mean to commit yourself to Christ? To what are you being committed? Concretely, what does it mean? As we taught in the Spirit Movement, it is not "grounded" anywhere. It does not touch real life experience anywhere. It is a feel-good abstraction masquerading as life's deepest religious truth. It leaves the worshiper without the possibility of rejoicing in the reality of his/her actual existence. It gets people gently free of the ontological responsibility of caring for the world in which they live. So in the more conservative churches salvation is rather crassly interpreted as "going to heaven", and in the more liberal churches, salvation is interpreted as being committed to Christ and thereby being a better

29

person with an unspoken promise of some kind of heavenly reward. In neither case is there a celebration of, or engagement in, the real world.

Actually this is the point at which we see most clearly the reason for the gradual decline of "mainline" protestant churches. Whereas the more fundamentalist churches can unabashedly preach the certainties of another world view, the more "respectable" mainline churches cannot quite bring themselves to do it. The fundamentalist churches hate the twentieth century tooth and nail and preach a condemnation of everything modern. (Yes, they do make exceptions for certain luxury items.) They give their people a context within which to embrace the thinking of a bygone age. Mainline churches do not have that luxury. They are filled with more educated and sophisticated people. A church in Greenville, S.C. this past Halloween created a "Judgement House". It was unabashedly designed to scare people with images of hell. It depicted a good person going to hell because she had not accepted Christ. It depicted a bad person going to heaven because he had accepted Christ while on death row. The "Judgement House" was a great success. Mainline churches, however, could not begin to get away with such tactics. My members cringed at the crudity of it. They may not have fully known how they disagreed with the theology, but they knew something was terribly wrong. So while the mainline churches are denied the ontological urgency of the "Judgement House", they have nothing with which to replace it. So the irony of it: The churches which are closer to the truth are losing ground to those who are furthest from it. The mainline churches are caught out in the no-man's-land between inability to embrace the old and unwillingness to embrace the new. In that land all the cats are grey and such is not the stuff of great sermons. There is only one hope for those of us who are caught in this dilemma: We must screw up our courage and embrace the truth. We will certainly take a hit, but in the long run I believe we will be all right. Of course we also have a strong element in our churches which wants us to join the fundamentalists. Is it any wonder that we are experiencing a good measure of divisiveness?

In 1987 my marriage of thirty years came to an end. The relationship had become a savage beast and in its dying throes was thrashing its tail around in deadly ways. We separated. The family belongings were sorted out. The children were crushed. The tears flowed. On one of those pain-filled days I fled to the ocean. I set my clock for pre-dawn and went to sleep. The next morning I was on the beach with my camera and tripod. I waited for sunrise and as I waited I said to the universe, "I need a miracle". I had a certain amount of confidence. I had tilted the playing field in my favor. Sunrise over the ocean had restored my sense of unity with the cosmos on countless occasions. Still I was unprepared for the miracle. The sun peeped over the horizon and a dolphin appeared in my view-finder. A dolphin! At the precise moment! That picture hangs in my office and is one of my symbols of the goodness of the Mystery. Of course, it was happenstance! Of course it had taken the Mystery some seventeen billion years to arrange that exact turn of events at precisely the moment when I needed it most. That dolphin and I are actually in the same family.

We are united. We were together in the original fireball. We were stardust together. It was a glorious reunion that morning at the beach. I was renewed. I knew that I would be all right. I was healed in the very deepest places of my soul. Now *that*, I contend, was an experience of salvation. There was no thought of Jesus or of some being called God. There was just the overwhelming experience of God's mysterious ways. Yes, I would say that what I experienced was the "Cosmic Christual".* The "Christ" that is the life-affirming nature of the universe itself, and that was certainly visible in the historical Jesus, was present that morning. That "Cosmic Christ" was in me and in the dolphin and in the ocean and in all creation. Indeed "...without him was not anything made that was made". (John 1:3 RSV)

That experience by the ocean did not delude me into pledging my allegiance to some abstraction. Rather, it bound me to the earth. My love for the oceans was increased. I became more concerned about the horrible pollution that is threatening them. My love for the beach increased. I was more likely to pick up a piece of trash as I walked back to my motel that day. I was more in love with dolphins than before and I have since tried to make a difference in matters of their survival. My experience of salvation bound me to the universe in a deeper and more caring way. At the same time I was a more whole person and was able to be more forgiving and more gentle in the days that followed. And I left the beach that day more in love with the Mystery than ever before.

Let me say it clearly: My experience has informed me that this universe in which I live is quite adequate. I have no yearning for transport to a "better place". Salvation is for me a very present thing. "Salvation has already come to my house." Yes, I might experience an even deeper unity with the Mystery tomorrow, but as of today I am quite convinced that I have not missed anything. When I walked into the Grand Canyon for the first time, I remember saying over and over again (as Native Americans taught me to say), "This would be a very good day to die". I knew I had been given the full gift. Yes, I know about heaven. It is here. It is right here! It would seem a betrayal of the giver of that wondrous gift if I were to long for something "better". Call it "realized eschatology" if you wish. Oh yes, the Mystery is not finished with me. I continue to experience newness in my salvation. But, paradoxically, I know already and for all time that I have not missed anything.

So what about "life after death"?

My dad lived until he was ninety. I loved him deeply. He was a model for me in many ways. He told me and showed me what the word integrity means. We shared a deep relationship. But when he died, I turned him loose. I have no yearnings to see him again in some distant place. I wished he could have been healthy and strong and lived for more years, but the universe is not constructed that way. Everyone gets old and dies. Dad received his full portion. To love life and its mysterious ways is to acknowledge the reality of death. Yes, and even to embrace

---

* See *The Coming of the Cosmic Christ* by Matthew Fox.

31

it.

But that is not quite the full picture. Every moment of life on this planet is clothed in eternity. When I am deeply at peace with the Eternal Center, I have a sense of eternity in the center of my being. It is "The Eternal Now", to use the title of Mr. Tillich's book. After all, what do we know about time and space? Scientists tell us that both were created with the original flaring forth of the universe. Does that not shake us loose from our easy (and too literal) pictures of eternal life? This salvation of which I speak is rich with eternality. We need not resort to ancient images from world views which have long since gone away.

And there is one more thing. My dad is with me in incredible ways. A few months ago I walked into some woods and as I entered the woods tears came to my eyes and a strange emptiness touched my stomach. It was Dad! He mysteriously encountered me in the place that he loved the most. His genes are in me. His emotional power lingers in me. His teachings are in me. He made a difference in the world and I live in that changed world. There is a sense in which it is true, as they say in Africa: "The dead are not dead". It is glorious and mysterious enough without any stretch of logic at all.

When I am asked serious questions by members of my congregation concerning "life after death", I respond this way: God is in charge of that. It is not mine to know. However, I trust God and know that the way God wants it is the way it is. That is quite enough for me. If the questioner is a hardy soul, I sometimes add the following: "If a person is going to church in order to get to heaven when s/he dies, then that person has missed the point". Quite. Even in the old cosmology.

We are not finished, though, with the question of salvation. We must consider a peculiar concept that is woven into the Christian tradition in the United States and most especially in the Southern part of that country. I refer to the concept of "Being Saved".

And I must admit that this is a difficult subject for me.

I was raised in the Bible Belt in a Pentecostal atmosphere. "Being Saved" was as normal a part of conversation as "pass the grits". Literally everyone that I knew at least gave lip service to "Being Saved". They might not have had the experience, but they certainly believed in its power and validity. It is unthinkable, even today, to question this cultural phenomenon in the midst of its adherents. It would be extremely painful.

In all the years since I left my Pentecostal connections, "Being Saved" has continued to be very present in the background. In my Methodist churches, there have been very few people who could testify about their own experience, but there has been almost no one who questioned the validity of it. There has even been some longing for it. That longing continues until today. Now and then someone in my church will say, "What we need is a good revival". We need to have some people get "Saved".

Even today when I am in a group of more conservative Christians and I hear them talking in the old language about how "Brother so and so got saved" and how

32

wonderful that was, I feel a deep tremor. Tapes from 'way back start playing and I wonder if my entire ministry has been off target. In addition, I have friends and relatives who would swear by the experience of getting "Saved" and who count that experience as the most important in their lives. I feel a need to apologize to them for the words that follow. I do not wish to do dishonor to them or to their spiritual journey.

Actually in the great epic of the Christian church, the practice of bringing people into the church via "Getting Saved" is relatively recent and brief. It is also mostly an American invention with roots in England and Germany. It had its heyday on the frontier. As a method of getting people into the church, it was quite successful in that setting. The population was very rootless. There were few established churches. Everything was new. The rule of law was somewhat tenuous. There were not many modes of entertainment. Have a big meeting, and get a bunch of folks saved. It was high drama and it worked.

Meanwhile the staid and stable churches (Episcopal, Lutheran, Catholic) tended to follow the old ways. Get the solid families into the church. Raise up their children in the proper ways and at the correct time confirm those children into the membership of the church. It had worked for centuries. Needless to say, these people tended to be the more affluent citizens. The old established churches did not object to the revivals. "Those people" needed some kind of church. It might also keep them from focusing too much on their low wages.

So the "Getting Saved" phenomenon tended to be limited to the poorer and less educated citizens. As "revival" churches grew and prospered and their members got higher up on the social scale, revivals tended to disappear. The United Methodist Church has deep roots in the revival tradition, but today receives almost no new members via the revival. Lip service is still given to the "Getting Saved" experience, but it is a rare event for someone to actually come down to the altar and "Get Saved". We United Methodists know very well today that we must build programs that will attract people to our churches. We build huge gymnasiums and hire recreational directors to make sure we have a "good program for the youth" since that is one of the major factors in choosing a church these days. One cannot imagine that during half time at the church basketball game the preacher would make an altar call. It is just not appropriate. We hope that these new people will someday "make a decision for Jesus", but we do not push that.

The technique for getting people saved was very set and fairly simple. First do a good attendance campaign. Be sure that you have a good crowd. Secure a good preacher who can preach with emotion and who can press for a decision. Begin the service with some good old-time music. The music is very important. It should bring back old emotional memories. It should remind people of early days in their own journey when maybe they themselves went down to the altar. We are talking the "old time religion" here. After a good "song service" the preacher takes over. First, s/he must convince any prospective convert in the congregation that s/he is a sinner and in danger of eternal damnation. This must get to be a very emotional issue. Then at the crucial point, offer the cure: Jesus. You can be forgiven of your sin and can be assured of a place among the saved while on earth and eternal bliss when you die. Many came down the aisles and acknowledged their sin and "accepted Jesus". It was very often a tearful and joyful moment.

So what can be wrong? Several things:

First, the concept of sin was very individualistic, and moralistic. The preacher had to condemn as "sin" what everybody already agreed upon as sin: drinking too much, cursing too much, being unfaithful in your marriage, and in some circles, smoking and dancing. It is, in the revivalist mentality, unthinkable repeat unthinkable to mention a serious social sin which might be controversial for the congregation. It would destroy the entire emotional climate which is needed for "Getting Saved". The preacher had to be careful. The sermon had to hit sin hard, but it had to hit sins that were "popular" with the crowd. Built into this plan, then, was this fatal weakness: Serious injustices could never be linked with the experience of becoming Christian. Never! I attended a four-day modern effort by the United Methodist Church to recreate a climate in which people might "Get Saved". The event occurred during the massive bombing of Iraq. The bombing was never mentioned. Our country was engaged in massive slaughter of relatively innocent people and for four days it was never mentioned. There was absolutely no mention of the war, not even in a prayer. One can imagine how successful a revival would have been on the frontier if the preacher had questioned our policies of genocide toward the Native Americans. The Christian church spread like wildfire across the prairie, but at a tremendous cost.

Second, the idea that a person must first be convicted of sin before being ready to receive Jesus is a very flawed idea. It is true that in order for a person to change, that person must first come to some awareness of the reality of his or her situation. Good therapy depends on this. A person is caught in a dilemma and feels helpless. The therapist helps him/her get a clear look at the real situation ("Yes, I did in fact mistreat my teenager.") and then change becomes possible. If a person is to be forgiven for a misdeed, that person must necessarily acknowledge the misdeed. But it is also possible for a person to be at a very good place, with a very healthy outlook and at that very moment experience a very close relationship with the Mystery. It is not necessary to convince a person that without Jesus her/his life is totally depraved. That emphasis is transparently an effort to force people into feeling a need for the solution the church offers. In fact, this preoccupation with sin has done much harm to the self-esteem of millions, while ironically, the great sins of our society were being ignored.

What we have then is an over-emphasis on a very individualistic notion of sin with an under-emphasis on the great issues of justice for all of God's creatures.

Third, the Jesus of the sawdust trail is a very truncated Jesus. He is very pious. He is hardly recognizable as the revolutionary figure we meet on the pages of the gospels. Jesus was crucified because he came out foursquare against drinkin' and cussin'? This truncated Jesus simply forgives and accepts people. But what about

Jesus' concern for the poor and the oppressed? What about his crossing over barriers that separate races and genders? What about his suggestion that we actually love our enemies? Even today you might hear a preacher admonishing the congregation that they must make sacrifices for Jesus, only to have the sacrifice turn out to be avoiding movies that have obscene language. I heard one well-known preacher admonish his people that they were a "peculiar" people. They were not like other folks. He then used as an illustration the fact that his neighbor was cutting his grass on Sunday morning while the good Christian people were driving to church.

Finally, I asked myself this question: When I have known people who "Got Saved", what difference did it make in their lives? I remember that usually they were on a kind of "high" for a few days or weeks. They were very excited about their experience and were quite willing to talk about it. Quite often this would result in increased activity in church. Sometimes the "Getting Saved" experience would result in a person joining a church, though more often the person would have already belonged to a church. Sometimes I have known a person to get free of a bad habit or addiction as a result of "Getting Saved". I would like to say that I have noticed a greater degree of self-esteem. I can't say that I have. I have sometimes noticed a greater tendency toward self-righteousness among such people. I have sometimes noticed an increased enthusiasm for fundamentalism and its various illusions. I have sometimes noticed a more vigorous hatred for people who are different. I have almost always noticed a greater concern for keeping the church focused on individualistic moral concerns. And in my thirty years of ordained ministry I have never known of a person who went through the "Getting Saved" experience outlined above who as a result became more committed to issues of social justice. Yes, I used the word "never".

REVELATION

To reiterate for a moment: We human ones have a glorious privilege. We are able to experience the incredible Mystery of the universe and give ourselves to it. This is the fullness of human-being-ness. It is a glorious and mystical experience. It is as common as the experience of looking at a beautiful sunset and saying "Ah". It can be as life-impacting as the experience of the disciples on the Mount of Transfiguration. It shakes us loose from our everydayness and puts us in touch with the dimension of life that is not subject to the clock. It refreshes us with the clean, pure water that flows from the fountain of life. Without this sense of unity with the Mystery our lives become very dry and shallow.

Strangely enough, we have a tendency toward that very dryness. Something in us fears the Mystery. The Unknown holds a fascination for us, but quite often the fear outweighs the fascination. So we escape. Our escapes often lead to horrendous results. We turn on each other. We turn on our own children. We may turn on our own bodies. We take this avoidance of Mystery methodology and make it the methodology of our living. We avoid truth wherever and whenever it is uncomfortable for us. So it is that when we turn our lives over to "sin" (escape from reality, or more commonly put, escape from God), it begins to rule our entire lives.

It will be no surprise to any of us that we have the above named tendency toward "hiding from God". It should also be no surprise that the most pleasant, albeit deadly, hiding place is the religious hiding place. If I can hide from God and call my hiding a religious virtue, then I have found a very comfortable illusion. Such a comfortable illusion pervades our present "culture religion". We refuse, steadfastly, to embrace the deep and wondrous Mystery of life and we use our religious beliefs and practices as a hiding place. Recently I attended a worship service in a very beautiful church. The stained glass windows were filled with rich symbolism. The problem was that no one in the entire building knew the meaning of the symbols. (Can you imagine the Marine Corps surrounding itself with symbols that have no meaning for the Corps?) The music and the hymns were beautifully performed, but they were filled with phrases and images that were unrelated to anyone's real life. The sermon was well prepared. It was well delivered. The preacher was one of the brightest and best. He focused on the "Kingdom of God". We are especially blessed, he said, because we are people of the kingdom. But what in the world is the "Kingdom of God"? Test the relevance of it in real life. Listen on the street. Do you ever hear the phrase in ordinary conversation among people who in fact do claim to be "people of the kingdom"? Ask any ten people in the pew next Sunday morning: "What is the Kingdom of God?" There will be only confusion. Yet, everyone assumes that the phrase is perfectly intelligible to the people. It is part of an elaborate code language that has long since ceased to speak of real life experience. Much of it is pious abstraction, far removed from everyday experience. The Bible is one main source of authority for this escapist religion. "Kingdom of God" is in the Bible, after all. Of course, we must know what it means!

But what is this Bible? And what is its relationship to the dilemma in which we find ourselves? Or how is it we come to experience and relate to the Mystery in a life-giving way? How does the Mystery "reveal" itself in our living. What is our understanding of revelation? In our traditional understanding of Christianity, there is no other place to begin except with the Bible.

One could imagine that a Holy Book might be of great value to us in our effort to stay close to Mystery. It should be written in our own world view. If it is written in another world view, it will lack power and will tempt us to consider its contents to be irrelevant to our time in history. It should be written with a constant invitation to face the unknown and indeed to welcome it into our hearts. There is a great temptation in us to pretend that we know what we don't know. We need holy instruction to help us avoid that trap. It should not claim for itself any special status which would tempt us to give allegiance to the book rather than to the Mystery. If it gives any specific moral instruction, that instruction should include the very best wisdom from our sages. It should not include any rules from ancient cultures which are no longer relevant or which reflect prejudices which we are trying to move

36

beyond. I say such a book might be of value to us. We, of course, do not have such a book.

We do have the Bible. Let's take a look at it with clear eyes. Let's look at it with the same critical eye that we might use if we were examining the holy writ of some other religion.

In the first place, it is written in the language and world view of a time long since gone. It easily accepts the pre-Copernican universe. It refers easily to Jesus being "taken up" into heaven (Acts 1:11). Later we can expect that "The Lord himself will descend from heaven..." (I Thes. 4:16) In the first century, that language made perfect sense. Today it does not. Yet we continue inside the portals of the church to use that language without clarification or translation. We go into the church and say, "Yes, the Lord will come down from Heaven". Then we go into the real world and know full well that there isn't any "Heaven" up there for anyone to come down from. There is just vast, deep space with countless galaxies spinning through it.

In the second place, the cultural situations in which the Bible was written are vastly different from our own. There is a record of God having some sons who perhaps were over-dosed on testosterone and were having sex with human women. God didn't like that kind of behavior, and put a stop to it. That, we are told, is why there are no giants in the land any more.(Gen.6:1-4) Where does such a statement come from? Why is such an absurd relic in the Bible? It comes from a very primitive time. One could excuse leaving it there, but one could not imagine that we would neglect to deal forthrightly with that kind of material in the Bible. Our people need to know that some of the Bible is far from "Holy".

Take a more familiar example: The conquest of Canaan. It is the "Promised Land". We can, of course, benefit from the metaphor of a people journeying toward a "Promised Land". There is value there. But historically, the Hebrew people had no right to simply move into someone else's land and drive the people out. How much tragedy has come to the Middle East because of that one illusion. God promised *us* this land, and that settles it! Today, in our "enlightened" time, that weapon continues to do its damage. How much influence this myth had on Europe as she set out to take over the entire world, we can only guess. Certainly, it was a very strong myth in the United States as we set out to claim our "promised land". And, what incredible cruelty! Saul shows a bit of mercy and does not kill the king. He follows "God's orders" and kills all the men, women and children, but he made the mistake of having a bit of mercy on the king and on some of the animals. God can't stand that kind of insubordination, we are told. Saul must pay a very big price, indeed, for his disobedience. (I Sam. 15:1ff) Should it be any surprise that a people raised on such stories would ride into Native American villages and slaughter men, women and children alike? If we insist on leaving such stories in our Bible, we should work very hard to clarify the situation for our people.

Take an even more common story: David and Goliath. We tell this story to every Sunday school student with great enthusiasm and with visual aids. What is

37

this story? It is a story of war, a story of killing. David has much in his life that we might use for spiritual instruction (for instance, his grief over Absalom's death), but most of our children only know the story about the killing of Goliath. We tell the story without apology. The great thing about our best Old Testament hero is that when he was just a boy, he killed a man. Does this do much to curb the tendency toward violence in our land? How much more of a hero David would have been if he had negotiated a truce with the enemy. I wonder if that has ever been included in a Sunday school lesson?

Consider the hatred for Baal and all his followers. In the Old Testament there was a great clash of cultures. Yahweh was on one side and Baal was on the other. The only press releases we get to read are the ones written by Yahweh's people. One of our favorite stories is the one about the contest on Mount Carmel. There we have an ancient rendition of the "Gunfight at the OK Corral". It is a fun story. It ends up with the slaughter of four hundred priests of Baal. Hear the applause from the congregation. Tell this story over and over again and watch the forces of Christendom slaughter the people of other religions all over this planet. This story is not what we need. We are trying to learn tolerance for all religions and at the same time we tell this ancient story without apology. Where are our brains?

Likewise as we seek to learn about gender equality and as we seek to root out the misogyny that prowls among us, the Bible is a mixed blessing. Read the story of Lot (Gen 19:8) and see how he considers his two virgin daughters to be available for bargaining chips as he seeks to placate a crowd. Read how Moses instructs his troops to kill all women of Midian who are not virgins and all the male children. But he thought it well to give to his troops the privilege of raping all the virgins. (Numbers 31:18) In the New Testament we are instructed to "Let a woman learn in silence with all submissiveness". (I Timothy 2:11) These various illustrations are perhaps excusable in their own context. What is not excusable is our unwillingness to forthrightly refute them.

Look now at our most pressing problem: The dying of the planet. We need a spirituality that will change the very deepest dispositions of Homo sapiens. Doing damage to the planet needs to gain taboo status somewhat akin to the present taboo concerning the consumption of human flesh. We need a revolution at the deeps of the spirit. Yes, it is true that the church is taking that task pretty lightly, but her Holy Book helps explain her reticence. The Bible offers a pretty consistent picture of a deity far removed from concern for the earth. Certainly, God is concerned for human beings (especially Hebrew ones), but it is rare to see a similar concern for the rest of the creation. While it is stressed that God created the earth and while now and then it is suggested that the creation speaks of God's glory, one searches long and hard to find any suggestion that the creation is itself sacred. Additionally, we are told that we human ones are to "subdue" the creation and to "have dominion" over all other creatures. (Genesis 1:28) Learned scholars are working hard now to find and to stress the Bible's ecological concern. Certainly part of the problem is the nomadic culture out of which the biblical heritage was born. Agricultural people are more likely to honor the earth than herdsmen are. And of course the arch-enemy in those early days was an agricultural people with a religion that openly related its faith to the fertility of the soil. Three thousand years ago we learned to hate any religion that honored the earth overmuch. We called them pagan. They have been open game for our warring parties even until today.

Closely related to the Bible's lack of concern for the earth is it's shameless anthropocentrism. Humans are the crowning achievement of the creation. (I suspect that if all species on the planet were to be given a vote only one would vote in agreement with that proposition.) Humans and their behavior are virtually God's only concern. It is said that people are created in God's "image" (Genesis 1:27) Scholars have tried to rescue that verse from the blatant stupidity with which it has been interpreted, but as far as the rank and file are concerned, it means that God looks like a human being. The extent of the anthropocentrism is illustrated by the fact that we can have serious arguments in the church concerning the gender of God. The danger of the anthropocentrism is illustrated by the incredible taken-for-granted rule that if the choice is between saving the environment or causing economic discomfort for human beings, human beings always come first.

I have preached from the Bible for thirty years. I take passages each week and find a way to relate them to real life. There are countless passages of scripture that I value very highly. The prophets of the eighth century B.C. are marvelous. The parables of Jesus contain some incredible wisdom. Paul's letters are filled with passages that will "preach". I am not advocating that we neglect those passages which clearly speak a word of truth no matter what the current cosmology. Rather I am begging for honesty about what the Bible really is. I am suggesting we glory in its gifts and face honestly its weaknesses and dangers.

My greatest appreciation for the Bible, however, is this: I believe that, in the midst of much confusion and in the midst of much misunderstanding and misuse, the Bible gives us permission to love life to the deeps. From the beginning where God says that the creation is "very good" (Gen.1:31), to the gospels where Jesus informs us that we are present to the deepest riches of God, I believe the Bible tells us that life is a very great gift and that we need only turn and receive it. Your life may seem like an arid desert, but you need only turn and touch the rock and you will find refreshing water. (Exod. 17:6) In spite of it all, the Bible contains the truth about life.

The real issue here, though, is not the Bible itself. The Bible makes no massive claim for itself. It is simply the record of a group of people through the course of about a thousand years who wrestled with life at sometimes very profound levels. They were, after all, the children of "he who wrestles with God". (Gen. 32:28) In the midst of that record can be discerned a "Remnant" of very deep and wondrous faith. Let it be that, and all is well. And perhaps we should get this said: The Bible does one thing that in our own time we seem very reluctant to do: It speaks its word of faith in its own world view and in the midst of its own cultural situation. It is faithful to its own times.

The real issue, then, is not the Bible itself. The real issue is our *treatment* of the Bible. We have elevated it to the status of "Paper Pope". We have indulged in the sin of "bibliolatry". We have done damage to the genuine value of the Bible by idolizing it. We have chosen to believe that the authors of the Bible were in some sense more than mere mortals. Somehow they were privy to the Mystery in ways that are not available to normal human beings. They were "inspired by God" as no one is today. I know not what rationale would inform us that more ancient people were closer to God than people in our own time. In so doing, we have separated our real living from the testimony of the Bible. People in those days, we say, were different from people in our day. Likewise we take the stories of various supernatural happenings as literal historical events. They are events that do not happen in our own experience, but we declare that they did happen in biblical days. Again, we are separated from the testimony of the Bible. It is obviously not very relevant to me. After all, I never saw a body alive after being dead for three days. Of course, this last criticism is not accurate for seminary professors. They have known the truth for a long time. Nonetheless, the truth in these matters has seldom reached the pew. One need only visit an adult Sunday school class in almost any church to be fully convinced.

As Joseph Matthews loved to say, "The Bible needs no defense. If you are defending the Bible, you can be sure you are in fact defending your own petty little illusion". Let the Bible simply stand (or fall) on its own. I believe it is capable of surviving without anyone's help. In fact, it might be of much greater worth if it could get free of some of its so-called friends. The issue, after all, is not the fate of the Bible. The issue is the fate of God's beautiful blue planet and all its living creatures. The issue is whether we human ones will continue to defy God, live in isolation, and kill the garden; or whether we will re-experience our oneness with the sacred Center and become co-workers with God.

When we come in due course to a discussion of the kind of spirituality which the new cosmology elicits among us I will go back to the Bible to show its value in illuminating the journey of the spirit. And when I come to the matter of justice I will reflect again on the incredible contribution the Bible has made to the entire human race's understanding in that area. For now having discussed at length the centerpiece of the Christian understanding of how it is that we might come into communion with the Mystery, let us look more broadly at that issue...the matter we traditionally call "revelation".

How does the Mystery reveal itself to humankind? One might also ask the question this way: How do we come to know the nature of the universe at its very deep and mysterious Center?

In seminary we were taught that the answer was this: Through the Bible! Or the answer might be expanded thusly: Through the events of history. Ours, it was said, is an historical religion. We believe that God makes him/herself known through the events of history. In the Old Testament, the event of primary revelation was the Exodus. In the New Testament the event was the crucifixion and resurrection of

Jesus. God chose those events for self-revelation. Since God is the Lord of History, we can learn of God by looking deeply at the events of human history. I say "human" history, since that seems to be the only history that we included. In practice the only history included was biblical history.

Yes, it is true that one can look at the Exodus and see that there is something in the midst of this universe that seems to be on the side of the quest for freedom. What is it that puts the yearning for freedom deep in the midst of our lives? The Mystery itself. In fact, we know that there is a deep yearning in the universe itself for the wild freedom of newness. The universe refuses to be fettered by the status quo. We can see that same truth in the movement toward freedom in the former Soviet Union, the feminist movement and the civil rights movement. The Exodus, then, is an illustration of how we learned something about the very nature of God through an historical event. Much more can be learned there, but this serves for purposes of illustration.

It is also true that we learn much about the nature of the Mystery at the cross and empty tomb. The primary lesson we learn is that the Mystery loves us very deeply. We are valued. We are valued to the point of death. A man gave himself up for the sake of a more human future for all humankind. In that event, we see the broader truth that we are all very important. Our lives are each of cosmic worth. The Mystery holds us dear. Realization of that truth can lead to a trust in the Mystery which can be life-transforming. So an historical* event reveals to us deep truths about the nature of the Center. More can be learned here, as well, but again this serves as illustration.

Of course! Of course God is revealed in historical events. After all, the Mystery is present bountifully in everything and in everybody and in every happening. The universe is filled to the brim with Mystery. Nothing could ever happen apart from it.

And it is appropriate that we single out some events as being especially helpful to us on our journey. My divorce was much more instructive to me than was my trip to the supermarket yesterday. Yes, it is quite possible that if I had been as attentive to the trip yesterday as I was to the divorce I might have learned even more at the supermarket. The actual fact remains that I look back to my divorce as a time when I touched the edge of Mystery in a very unique way. My life was greatly changed by it. It was during that time, for instance, that I started writing poetry. The Mystery makes itself known to us through the events of history.

There are two questions that must be raised. First, why have we limited history to human history? Human beings have only been aboard the space ship for about (at most) three million years and at anything resembling our present state of

---

* By "historical" I do not mean to imply that the resurrection of Jesus was literal. Rather I mean that new life happened among the followers of Jesus. We call the experience of life emerging from deadness "resurrection".

41

development probably less than one hundred thousand years. The universe has been in process for about seventeen billion years (give or take a few billion). As we discern the journey of the universe for those billions of years, are we not likely to be instructed about the ways of the Mystery? Is it not even quite conceivable that we might learn something from all of those billions of years that dwarfs anything we have learned from our few thousand years of recorded Judeo-Christian tradition? Fear not! It is the Mystery that we follow. What if our pursuit of Mystery were to shake loose some of our cherished dogma? It would only mean that the Mystery was following its relentless march toward the new. Nothing stands in its way. Certainly our little human dogma will not prevail against it.

And what about the other creatures? And what about the mountains and the sea? What about the flowers and the stars? They, too, have a history. They, too, are happenings. Do they not have the privilege of informing us about the Mystery? Admittedly, there have been countless saints down through the ages of our tradition who have contended that God is revealed in all of nature. In my own training, however, I was told that God was revealed only in human history. Sometimes I was told that only in the Christ-Event could I learn anything reliable about God. It has been my experience that in the Christian church at large, this same line has been followed. It is said in different ways: "Only the Bible tells us about God", or "Only in Jesus Christ do we know the Father", or "Outside the Church there is no salvation."

As I have suggested, such has not been my experience. In fact, quite the opposite. My most profound and informative experiences of Mystery have been outside the confines of the Christian bailiwick. My experiences have not been at odds with the central learning of the cross as discussed above, but they have been more powerful for me and more life-altering. Had I confined my learning to the Christ-Event itself, my life would have been immeasurably poorer. Let me say it differently: If I had encountered the Cosmic Christ only in the biblical story of Jesus, I would have been much the poorer. Thankfully, the Cosmic Christ has chosen to touch and teach me through the wonder of the entire universe.

The second question is this: Why do we value secondary revelation so highly when primary revelation is readily available? When we read the story of the Exodus, we are reading a very second-hand version. We are not experiencing the Exodus itself. Yes, the Jews work very hard to re-experience the Exodus as they celebrate it, but it is still an event which happened in the distant past. In addition, the rich theology of the Exodus is all second-hand. For the most part, the faithful are simply told of the Exodus and are told its meaning. The Christ-Event is likewise a history for which we ourselves were not present. We are taught its meaning. Hopefully, we experience its meaning at a very deep level. Still, it is not history of our own life experience. Some other people had this experience. It was very important to them. They felt that the Mystery was revealed to them in the experience. They wrote about the experience. We read about it and learn about the Mystery in the process. It is second-hand revelation.

It is this problem which leads us to emphasize the importance of "experiencing Jesus Christ in a very personal way." Sometimes, people do receive that kind of personal experience. One might ask whether the Jesus Christ of their experience is similar at all to the Jesus of the Gospels, but still it is often very powerful and meaningful. However, in the church as I have known it, that kind of powerful and meaningful experience of Christ has been rare in people's lives. The revelation of the Mystery in the Christ-Event remains for most people a very second-hand revelation. We believe it. We accept it. We honor it. But it did not happen in our lives.*

Meanwhile, the Mystery is very much at hand. It is upon us! It is "within" us. We need only open our eyes and LO, it is there! I see cascades of dogwood blossoms across my back yard and LO it is there! I walk into the Grand Canyon and am aware of the Mystery. I am in a group of people and we are working on our journeys. One of our number is struggling hard with some buried pain. Finally, out of nowhere s/he summons up the courage to confront that pain in our midst. Awe sweeps through the room. As Carlyle Marney would have put it, "I think we just had church." It is the Mystery. It is everywhere present. It supports me. It makes me know that I am valued. It deepens my love for life. It is life-changing. *And it is first-hand.* No one is telling me about it. No ancient saints are explaining it to me. It is simply happening in my own life. As a matter of fact, I count that as my inalienable right! I have a right to experience God myself! I have a right to experience it the way I experience it without anyone else standing between me and the experience! I am my own priest!

One can understand the church's reluctance to turn people loose to simply experience God on their own. Where is the control? What if a person actually *is* "closer to God" on the proverbial golf course? Where is the authority of the church? I read in the confirmation ritual that all people stand in need of that which the church alone supplies. Who says so? The church itself says so. The church also is afraid not to say so. If we do not have some control on people's access to the Mystery, they might simply do their own accessing.

It should be noted here that the Cartesian mentality of recent centuries contributed mightily to the church's confusion at this point. The western world was falling head over heels in love with the left brain. Rational thought was the solution to every mystery and the answer to every question. It is not surprising that the church trusted human philosophy and theology more than she trusted the Mystery. Rational thought also affords the church a great deal of control. I spent several years on the Board of Ordained Ministry in our conference of the United Methodist Church. It was our task to screen and finally approve or disapprove applicants for

---

* I shall discuss later the need for a powerful mythology which can be rehearsed and ritualized among a people to help them relate in a life giving way to the Mystery.

the ministry. We required written proof that they understood and subscribed to our notions of Christian theology. It was all shamelessly left brain. One might have them write a poem, paint a painting, tell a story, or describe a moment of awe. It never crossed our minds. We require our ministers to be pre-occupied with the rational, analytical aspect of life. It is the way we ourselves were trained. It is also a preferred method of control.

Actually, I think we need not be so fearful. People who have encountered the Mystery in a first-hand fashion have a great love for sharing that experience with others. They love to hear of the experiences of others. They feel a need to be reminded of the Mystery and its primacy in life. They search for comrades in their battles to combat oppression and to save the earth. They almost invariably turn toward community. It would not destroy the church were she to acknowledge the instant availability of the Mystery to "all of every age and station" quite apart from any particular beliefs and/or practices. After all, as Jesus made clear to Nicodemus, this is a birth from the Mystery itself. (John 3:3) It is not a thing that anyone should seek to control.

It is not necessary to deny the time-honored tradition about God being revealed in history. (You could say that there isn't anything else...just as you could say there isn't anything else but nature.) I just want my own personal history to also be included. And I want the history of the entire creation to be included. Who has the authority to decide that only this or that historical event is worthy of consideration? Oh yes, I am aware of the various dangers of allowing folks to venture into the Unknown on their own and to even trust their own history (experience). I am also aware that if a person has the courage to make that venture there is no pope or bishop with the power to stand in the way. And I have seen the cost of having folks live at distance from the Mystery and its life-giving power. I will discuss that cost next.

CHAPTER FOUR

THE COSTS AND THE PAY-OFFS OF ILLUSION

We have seen the "Great Separation" up close. The dominant religion of our culture is mired in a very out-dated cosmology and is shackled to old metaphors and images which are not only rooted in the old cosmology but which are treated as literal renderings of historical events. We are deprived of a spirituality which could help us relate to our own era and we are deprived of the wisdom which might come to us through the metaphors of an ancient time. Thus we are very separated from the Holy Mystery which...we have reason to believe...could provide us with refreshment.

At the same time we notice that we are living amidst great chaos. It seems like almost everything that used to be nailed down is coming loose. Racism ravages our planet. Militarism wipes out the economies of countless nations. Crime is rampant in the United States. The environment is being assaulted by an insatiable drive for economic growth which in turn is driven by an almost obscene consumerism. The poor across the planet as well as in the United States are getting poorer and the rich are getting richer and the poor are being blamed more than ever for being poor. Is it not self-evident that there must be some deep place where all these maladies come together...some problem that lies deep enough to be at the root of the tree? What is the connection between crime and environmental destruction and consumerism? Is it not a spiritual matter? Does it not have to do with our grasp of the significance of the cosmos?

Why then do we continue to keep on keeping on in our old ways? In this chapter, I hope to give a little bit of a clue as to what the payoff is for our inaction. Then I want to reinforce my argument for a new spirituality by pointing to the cost of our lethargy. I believe we are getting a very comfortable payoff for living in illusion and for that reason we avoid the spiritual revolution that is necessary and which in the long run might save our planet. I believe the illusion has us blinded to the very high price that we are paying for inaction. First, let us consider the payoff.

I heard our president recently say in a press conference that ours is the most religious of the industrialized nations. We go to church. We speak of church-going as a virtue even if we do not go ourselves. It is evident that, for all its problems, we do love our religion. I should make clear that I am speaking of Christianity. We are not so in love with Buddhism or Islam. We are especially not in love with the off-beat brand of Christianity that manages to break through all the difficulties and speak a prophetic word. What we love is the comfortable "culture religion" to which we are wedded.

Note the inscription on our money: "In God We Trust." If there is any reality in the universe which we, as a nation, have no intention of trusting, that reality is God. However, we do have a major idol which we *do* trust. We trust it heart, mind and soul. It is no accident that we chose that particular idol for the inscription. We trust money (material accumulation) arguably more than any other people in the world and we put on our money the words "In God We Trust." Isn't that a nice touch? Surely somewhere in the higher levels of Wall Street someone now and then has a belly laugh over this. And it actually seems to work. It seems good and appropriate to the masses of Americans that the inscription be where it is. We love our religion. Even our God submits to our manipulations.

In my youth I recited the pledge to the flag without major reservations. The pledge was without religious taint. Of course it did have in it that business about "liberty and justice for all" when a large portion of our population was not allowed to vote and was even in constant danger of being lynched, but at least it did not claim God's blessing. Alas, before long our congress got the idea of adding the words "under God" to the pledge. What a nice pious touch. Our nation is under God. We are a God-fearing nation. Maybe we are even God's chosen people. What a convenient religion that goes along so happily with national hypocrisy. No wonder we love our religion so much.

Listen to the argument about prayer in public schools. Surely if such a great portion of our people want to have prayer in our public schools, we must be a religious people. No matter that almost no offices or factories begin their day with prayer. Forget that. We are serious about prayer in public schools. We are about ready to circumnavigate the Bill of Rights to get it done. What, one wonders, does anyone expect these prayers to accomplish? What if the teacher led the children in a prayer which implored God to free us from our militarism, our racism or our homophobia? What if the prayer dealt with our real lives and our real injustices? In other words, what if the prayer turned out to be *real* prayer? If one is familiar with the docile role that religion plays in our country, one will find that last scenario almost impossible to imagine. We love our religion because it can usually be trusted to bless the status quo.

Why do we love our religion so much? There are three reasons which stand out: 1) It is irrelevant, 2) It is escapist, and 3) It feels good.

Why would we continue for centuries into a new world-view using the categories of an ancient world-view for our religion. We use the categories of that ancient world-view in no other facet of our living, but we cling to them in our religion. Why do we continue to pledge allegiance to a "Supreme Being" in the sky when our world view has long since made such an image irrational? The reason might be this: Such a far off and irrational being can make no claim on us. It can make only a minimal difference in our living. And such an imaginary being can be manipulated very easily. If we are in competition with the earth religions of Europe, we can get such a being to give us permission to kill several hundred thousand witches. If we need our homophobia supported, we can readily get our distant god to go along with our prejudice. If we decide to institute a national policy of genocide toward the indigenous population of this continent, we can count on our God not to raise a ruckus. This being in the sky is not seriously related to the real issues of our lives. We enjoy the irrelevancy.

Why would we persevere in teaching a concept of sin that is so puny as to convict almost no one. We have moved little from the days of my childhood when sin was "dancing, cussing, drinking, and inappropriately sexual intercoursing." We have decided that dancing might after all be OK, but our understanding of sin continues to be puny. Again, it is not accidental. When a country is founded on the enslavement of one non-white race and the genocide of another non-white race it is necessary to try some diversionary tactic. Focusing on cussing and drinking might seem a bit too obvious, but only to those who live outside the illusion. Even today it would be a rare day in church when sin included such meaty items as militarism, economic imperialism, racism, consumerism, and homophobia.

Our religion is comfortably irrelevant in addition because its ethics are so thoroughly individualized. How a religion so closely related to the Hebrew prophets could get to be so unrelated to social issues is difficult to fathom. Perhaps it was because we so desperately *needed* a religion that was irrelevant. How does one go to church on Sunday when one is participating in the institution of slavery or segregation or genocide? It would be a painful experience unless your church was domesticated to the point where it would mention only individual sins which were divorced from the social fabric. It would also help if you could go to church and hear about some sin of which you were totally innocent. You could go home feeling pretty good. I grew up in an area where profanity was considered "low class." I never used profanity because I did not want to be considered "trash." When the preacher condemned profanity I was clean. I still hear main-stream preachers preaching against profanity in movies. Hollywood, as everyone knows, is a din of iniquity. I don't make movies, so I am still innocent.

Another contributing factor to the irrelevance is the fact that the minister/leader is hired by the people s/he serves. The sermons/teachings must be fairly comfortable for the people to hear or they will hire someone else. We can assume that we are all living godly lives. Our preacher has not told us otherwise. And if our preacher did tell us otherwise, we would get another preacher. Ministers, like most folks, have to make a living. It may also be true that most ministers, by the time they leave seminary, are pretty thoroughly domesticated. They might have a clue about the "Great Separation", but they have been taught to keep it quiet. The people in the pews are not yet ready to hear such radical notions.

The second reason we love our religion is because our religion is escapist. As I have pointed out earlier, for the great majority of Christians, our religion is about getting to heaven when we die. This is a little confusing, because there seems to be almost no existential concern for actually going to heaven. Lives are not being shaped by that concern. I encounter almost no one who is trembling about the issue of facing the "Great Judgement Day." Therefore we might assume a kind of universal awareness that such concerns do not mesh well with our current cosmology. Nevertheless I believe the old picture of "going to heaven when we die" serves an important function in our culture. It helps us avoid the application of the faith to the genuinely difficult struggles of contemporary living. Our religion after all is not primarily concerned with this world. It is primarily concerned with life in another place. The difficult teachings of the Bible, therefore, need not be taken too seriously. They are meant in a "spiritual sense." In the popular mind that generally means they are not intended to deal with actual conflicts in this world. Preachers should stick to "spiritual" matters. They should not stick their noses into controversial issues. It is hard to imagine a more convenient religion than that. The reality of our situation is that our religion is helping us to escape the Mystery's call. Our religion is helping us to hide from God.

The third reason we love our religion so much is because it makes us feel good. It makes us feel that we ourselves are good. It offers us "cheap grace" which allows us to feel good about ourselves without confronting our complicity in the cruelty and injustice and planetary destruction of our time. Listen to some one who has been to church on Sunday morning. She might say, "I feel like I have been to church." That means the worship service contained nothing deeply disturbing. It made the worshipers feel good about how they were living their lives. As a worshiper, I might have been challenged to make some minor improvements: Love my husband more, be a better parent, teach a Sunday school class, etc.; but I did not have to question any of my deep prejudices. Certainly, "I do not go to church to hear politics discussed!" Translation: I do not want church to deal with the painful issues of society. I want to leave church feeling good. In my ministry, I have found the most dangerous criticism to be this one: "I leave church feeling all churned up inside." In this country, most churches manage to have people leave church feeling good. This is one of the most common benefits of, and reasons for, living in illusion.

In addition to the above problems with our religion it is also true that many people are helped in a personal way by their church and by their faith. Not long ago I visited a very old woman who was facing life-threatening surgery. She did in fact die a few weeks later. She said to me that day: "The Lord has always taken care of me and I guess He will now." I could see that she was receiving real comfort from that confidence. It was her way of trusting the Mystery. I honor that very deeply. Quite often a parishioner will say to me that my sermon really touched her/his life. "It was like you knew exactly what was going on in my life." I believe that such personal help is quite often provided by the church. The church fellowship itself is quite often very helpful. I notice people being really caring toward each other in the women's groups or in the Sunday school classes. Basic human care is extended through the structures of the church. Such benefits would certainly be enhanced by a more relevant spirituality.

Now let us turn to the price we pay for "The Great Separation".

The people who work in the field of addiction have an image that I find helpful here. It is the image of the elephant in the living room. The addiction is the elephant. It is right there in the living room, but no one talks about it. Everyone carefully avoids mentioning it. It is a family secret and everyone conspires to keep the secret. But there is a problem: The family pays a very high price indeed for the elephant and for the conspiracy of silence.

We, in the Christian west and especially in the United States, have an elephant in our living room. Our dominant religious tradition is caught in the cobwebs of a bygone age. Its images and metaphors and its taken-for-granted view of the universe are all mired in that ancient age. We live in an age that for the past few decades has changed immeasurably. Many books have been written about that one fact alone: The accelerated rate of change. The picture that we carry in our heads about the way the universe is constructed is radically new. The rate of change is continuing to accelerate. Incredibly, Christian preachings and teachings have changed almost none at all. Rudolf Bultmann did some magnificent work on the New Testament. His goal was to help us de-mythologize the Bible. He wanted to help us get back to the life issues inside the ancient metaphors. Where could one look today, half a century later, for signs that his work was of benefit to the church? Other theologians have labored at the task. The results in the church at large have been negligible. We still use the old images and metaphors without apology and without a hint that they are not related to the real world in which we live. The elephant is still in the living room and there is still a conspiracy of silence in the church.

We, as a society, are paying a very high price indeed for the elephant.

In the first place, in the absence of any deep immersion in the wonder of the creation itself our people are seeking ecstasy in all the wrong places. What is this crass consumerism about? Is it not a search for some kind of a "high"? Is it not almost beyond belief that any society would find "shopping" to be recreational? How could anyone in a world such as ours justify our consumerism? Is it not the opposite of the central message of Jesus' ministry? Raise children on the ecstasy of shopping and see how they turn out. Notice the addiction to violence among us. We are reduced to getting our ecstasy from watching a car explode on the TV set or a body being torn apart by bullets. Of course we have alcohol and drug problems. We are separated from the natural ecstasies of life and are compensating in weird and destructive ways.

Life is full and rich when it is immersed on a regular basis in the glorious mysteries of the universe itself. (If you wish, you can read that as "immersed in God".) Our religion has the task of at least reminding us of that possibility. Our religion does not do that. It would be better if it were not for the silence. We could simply be up front about it and say, "Hey, we have failed. We no longer lead people into the ecstatic center of life. You are on your own." In that case, people might flock to the mountains and the gardens and the seashore and the telescopes for their own experiences of wonder. Needless to say, we have not acknowledged our failure. We continue to promise people that we will care for their spiritual needs when in fact we are not prepared to do so. Where would you go to find a group of people who were the least likely to experience ecstasy? I suggest the normal eleven o'clock worship service on Sunday morning. People might learn something there. They might be helped in some struggle or other. But ecstasy? Just look at their faces about half-way through the service and you will know. The proof of what I say is that they leave church and go shopping (!) to get some kind of a high. Jesus accused the scribes and Pharisees of refusing to enter the kingdom themselves and of not allowing others to enter (Matthew 23:13). We religious leaders of this day are equally guilty. We are sincere. We feel it is a service to the church (and not incidentally to our own careers) to keep the silence. Meanwhile, the people who trust us are living in isolation from the Holy Center of the Cosmos itself.

In the second place our nation(s) lives without a viable conscience. In any social unit there needs to be a voice that speaks for the deeps of life. It needs to be a voice that has at least some measure of independence from the powers that silence dissent. It is assumed that the religious structures of a society will perform that function. If not the church, then who? Shall we turn to the State Department? Or to Sears? Or to CBS News? Who will call us back to the pathways of justice and righteousness when we go astray? Yet in our society, the church (with a few glorious exceptions) does not function as a conscience for the society or for the nation. There are two ways in which the conscience function could be imagined. If people are led down into the mysterious depths of life where they experience the unity and interdependence of all things, they will come back much more committed to "justice for all" and much less committed to "justice for us and to hell with the rest." The other possibility would be for the leaders of the church to speak courageously to the faithful with freedom and with justice for all on their hearts. Neither of these happen in the normal life of our church. Again the tragedy is amplified by the fact that it is assumed by the populace that our church is functioning as our conscience. The result is that our religion baptizes our nation's every sinful impulse.

I went to Nicaragua during the contra war. I went into the countryside and into the "war zone." I talked to peasants who had a very firsthand experience of the war. I learned that our country was financing a war of assassination and terror. All war has some horror in it, but this war had assassination and terror at the very center of its strategy. Our nation was paying for the systematic torture and murder of Nicaragua's civilian population as a strategy for undermining the government of Nicaragua. This was not a secret. Thousands of solid citizens from our country went to Nicaragua and learned what I learned. Where was the voice of the church in this country? There were, of course, a few ministers across the land who tried to communicate the truth to their people, but in the vast majority of churches the issue was never mentioned. Our Conference paper in South Carolina Methodism declined to publish the report that our delegation submitted. The national publications of United Methodism were silent. If the churches were quiet about the war, would it not seem reasonable to assume that the war was just? (I hasten to say that there were small groups of Christians who were heroic in their opposition to that war. Witness for Peace is the one with which I am most familiar.)

More recently, in a kind of national spasm, our dark side took over for a few weeks and propelled us into the Persian Gulf War. It was perhaps history's best

50

illustration of enormous casualties combined with a poor rationale for war. From the very beginning one could feel our country getting ready for a stupendous release of pent up frustration and self-doubt. The nation of Iraq was both small enough and scary enough to make a perfect scapegoat. We unleashed all our frenzy and killed a hundred and fifty thousand people. We contributed directly to thousands of additional deaths due to disease. As the war ended our entire nation erupted in joyous celebration. Where was the church in this? Where was our national conscience? Where was a little humane concern for the thousands of dead? At a two thousand member United Methodist Church near my town they handed out American flags at the morning worship service and the pastor compared Jesus favorably to "Stormin' Norman".

Finally, we are paying a very high price for our religion's separation from the creation itself. As I have shown, Yahweh was never much of a lover of the earth. He did create it, but it seems that He lost interest in it. We get hints that Jesus was very much of a lover of the earth, but by the time we got the record through the Greek censors, we had lost much of that emphasis. And by the time the gospel got through Platonism, Stoicism, Gnosticism, and the Cartesian mentality, we certainly had little left in it that would honor the earth. The times have changed and once again the Mystery is being encountered right in the midst of the natural world, but our religion is blissfully unaware. The most rational of scientists in our time are being "blown away" by the Mystery that is at the universe's center. People are indeed turning toward the creation itself to experience the "Creator." But our religion continues to tell people that the Mystery is best experienced in the stories and rituals of long ago. Sometimes our religion even warns people that nature is evil and untrustworthy as a point of encounter with the Mystery.

Consequently, we are of little help in the struggle to save the earth. Almost all indicators are indicating the declining health of our Mother Earth. She is being crucified beneath our feet. We are all implicated. We all profit...in the short term...from her destruction. We need a spirituality among us which helps us to honor her health. Otherwise we will all simply perish together.

Such is the price our society pays for our addiction. The fabric of our common life is coming unraveled as our people search for significance in all the wrong places. Our nation runs amuck among the poverty-stricken people of the world, killing them without remorse and "helping them" in death-dealing ways. Most serious of all, the creation itself is at risk and we in the church are still speaking about nature as if it were our enemy. Our pet elephant is indeed an expensive one.

Certainly such societal costs are very high. Indeed, words fail us at points of such ontological gravity. How does one express the danger of losing the health of our planet? Yet, the cost does not stop there. Each of us individually pays a price in terms of our interior life.

The "Great Separation" leaves each of us living in a very dry land. A land where holiness seems distant, where miracles seem not to happen, where our lives seem isolated, and where communion with God seems impossible. Let us consider each of these maladies in turn.

We live in a place where holiness seems absent. We have cut ourselves off from the sense of the holiness of all life and now we must live without a sense of the holy. That by itself is a tragedy of massive proportions. Perhaps we can understand how it happened. In reaction against massive superstition, and in pursuit of truth, our ancestors abandoned any appreciation for the holy in life. There just wasn't a place for it in their plan. Then in euphoric allegiance to the industrial revolution and the growth of capitalism they were quite willing to rape and pillage the earth and its living creatures. Such a conquest was profitable and was served quite well by a non-sacred universe. We can understand that, even if we are not able to appreciate it, but it left us in a very dry place.

How does one live without the wonderful experience of the holy in the midst of one's actual every-day life? Has there ever been a time in human history when we were so separated from the Mystery and depth of life itself? What does one do to compensate? Take drugs? Go shopping? Drive a fast car? Become addicted to work? Go to war? Of course. We live in such a dry place.

I am not suggesting that we human beings in our weakness have to pretend that life is holy in order to avoid drugs or war. No. The truth is that life IS holy! We live in a time when the holiness, the mysteriousness, the depth, and the wonder of life are more obvious than perhaps ever before in history. Certainly we have this plus: We have come to the awareness of the holiness of life on the far side of unbridled scientific inquiry. We are not having to pretend about anything. We are not having to defend ourselves against anybody's newest theory. The simple truth is that when the best minds of our day get to the TRUTH as best they can discern it, they discover it to be utterly mysterious. I think the people most likely in our time to be really in touch with awe are the sub-atomic physicists. It was not the fundamentalists with their fear of the truth who led us back to the holy. It was the fearless followers of truth who followed that light until it set them free. Ahhhh. Yes, reality is of God and for that reason need never be feared.

We live in a dry land where no miracles seem to happen. We acknowledge that miracles did happen in olden days. We read about them in the Bible. People rose from the dead! They walked on water! They caused water to flow from rocks! They could even stop the sun, if necessary, to win a battle. Those were the days. But alas, times are different now. Have you ever seen a miracle? Tell me about it. Oh yes, we all know about the religious con men who hatch up miracles in order to make money. But really now, have you ever seen a miracle? How sad to live in a time when there is no sense of the miraculous. What a dry place.

But in the real world, it is not that way at all. Here is the wonder of it: We live in a universe where miracles happen in the commonplace. It is not a matter of trying to get some miracle to happen. ("Send me a hundred dollars and I will get God to perform a miracle for you.") Thank God we have passed those dreary days. It is now a matter of simply having the eyes to see the miraculous before your very eyes. All of life is so incredibly full-of-wonder that you can see a miracle anytime you are able to open your eyes. Start any place you want to. Consider the pancreas. Not only is it able to manufacture precisely the chemical that your body needs to handle sugar, but it is able to monitor its distribution into the blood stream with incredible accuracy. What a miracle! Watch two thousand birds rise from the ground at precisely the same moment. Miraculous. Watch the great sea turtle find the same tiny island in the ocean year after year without any map and without any satellite assistance. How marvelous it is to be aware of a miracle. What a glorious "high" that is. How sad that our religion itself has helped to isolate us from the true nature of the world which we inhabit.

I think it was fear that did it. It seems that religious folk wanted desperately to believe the miracles of the Bible and were afraid that someone would "explain them away" or discredit them in some way. This made them always expect miracles to be supernatural...some kind of disruption of the natural. It was even connected to confidence in the ability of God. "If someone is proven to have cancer and then the cancer disappears, I will believe in God." "If I can believe that Jesus actually rose from the dead, then I will be more likely to believe in God." Conversely, if I were to lose my belief in the miracles of the Bible, I might at the same time lose my belief in God. So we held on tightly to a "supernatural" view of miracles and since we did not see any supernatural events in our own lives, the entire experience of the miraculous was lost. It is a sad business. We were led to believe an unreal interpretation of the Bible and were thereby cut off from the "real life" that the Bible is in fact about and as a consequence were cut off from the depth and wonder of our own existence.

We live in a dry place where our own lives are not related to the larger enterprise of the universe. There is, in the normal (Christian or non-Christian) person's life little awareness of being a part of the future of the universe. There is little sense of "call." We do have this tradition of religious leaders being "called" by God to the ministry. One is tempted to ask, given the irrelevance of the church, what kind of a God would be spending time calling people into it's middle-class, comfortable, unaware leadership. But aside from the narrow and somewhat suspect arena of "Christian vocation", few people have a way of seeing themselves as deeply in harmony with the development of the universe itself. It is a dry place. Is my life not related to anything larger than getting my kids through college?

But again, our religion is contradicting reality. The truth is that we are, all of us, vitally connected to the entire universe. If Dr. Einstein taught us anything at all, he taught us that. More than ever before we can understand ourselves as vitally connected to the work of "God." It is not some magic event. It is just the way it is. And then as one gets into a close relationship with the holy and begins to grasp the glory of it, one can in fact begin to feel the pulling and tugging of the furthest galaxy as it seeks to bend our will toward the health of its stars. The sense of "call" is not such a puny thing as we have thought. It has to do with one's participation in the grand and glorious work of the universe itself at it's Holy Center. How sad it would be if such a glorious experience were denied the common people. And how very sad if it were relegated to a group of people who are perhaps most removed from reality and who have sold their birthright in this time of crisis.

The dryness of our time is further demonstrated by the fact that we have little sense of "salvation." We have little sense of being in a close relationship with God. At best, some of us might imagine ourselves to be in a close relationship with a "Father" in some distant place. I contend that while such a relationship might provide some solace and even guidance, it actually stands in the way of a relationship with the Mysterious Center of this universe. I believe that, for most of us, our religion's ancient images stand in our way and contribute to the dryness of our times. Our story is something like this: We commit our lives to God at some point in our lives. We don't have much of a clue as to what we mean by the word "God", but it seemed good to make the commitment. Are we experiencing "Salvation"? What would we mean by that word? Salvation, we were taught, means that we will "go to heaven" when we die. There we will experience closeness with God and will be able to "walk and talk with Jesus." We are told that we should in the meantime live in a personal relationship with Jesus, but since that entire scenario seems so far removed from the real world that we inhabit, we necessarily find ourselves living in a very dry place.

Thank God, it doesn't have to be so. It is possible to live in a close and holy relationship with the Mystery of life. We are in fact as intimately related to that Mystery as the human mind could ever conceive. The secret is not to try to emulate some religious pattern of conversion, but to simply turn loose the defenses that protect us from the awareness of the Mystery. We can stop all our diversionary tactics: Accumulation of wealth, patriotism, drugs, work, etc. We can simply let ourselves go. As the fish lives in the water, we live in the Mystery. Embracing the reality of that relationship is the secret. It is a good and fulfilling way to live. "Our hearts are restless" when we live otherwise.

We live in a dry place. We are led by a tradition that in ancient times was able to lead people to water. Ironically, that very tradition has forgotten how to find the water. It thinks it sees the water and it claims to be leading people to it. Alas, the water is only a mirage and our thirst continues. Our Christian guides are wedded to their illusions and as of now are not willing to break free. In spite of all that, the good news remains: The Water is right here beneath our feet. We come now to consider that Water.

CHAPTER FIVE

THE EMERGING SPIRITUALITY

We come now to consider the qualities of that new spirituality which seems to be emerging among us. These qualities certainly describe my own spirituality as it has been developing over the past several decades, but I learned them from much greater life than my own. I learned them from the times in which I live. I learned them from Matthew Fox and Joseph Campbell and Loren Eiseley and Annie Dillard and Fritjof Capra and from the Cosmos itself. These qualities seem to me "self-evident" as we consider a spirituality appropriate for the age in which we live: We need a spirituality which enhances the present moment in which we live. We need a spirituality which is rooted in reality. We need a spirituality which honors our interdependence. And we need a spirituality which is capable of producing a new mythology for the communication of truths too deep for analytical explanations.

HERE AND NOW

There was a popular song a few years ago that had in it this refrain: "Is that all there is?" Having had various experiences of life, the songwriter asked that question again and again. Is this all there is to life? Am I missing something?

There is the sunrise over the ocean. There is the yawning grandeur of the Grand Canyon. There is the magnificent beauty of the azaleas in the spring. There is the delight of young kittens playing in the sun. There is the birth of one's first child. There is the taste of a nice cantaloupe in the summer. There is the experience of being in love. There is sexual ecstasy. There is the capacity to shed tears for someone else's pain. There is the splendor of Orion on a brisk fall night. There is the great humpback whale making its music in the deeps. There is beauty and wonder and splendor and Mystery. And I am gonna ask "Is that all there is?" Well, the answer is "Yes, that is all there is."

This spirituality which now asks for our attention will be a wondrous thing indeed. It will be appropriate for the Einsteinian cosmology. It will be firmly rooted in reality. There will be no pretending necessary. There will be no abstract requirements made of it's adherents. It will be based on the indicative, not the imperative. It will be available to all. No esoteric skills of meditation will be required. It is as clear as the next raindrop and it as mysterious as the origin of time and space. It is thoroughly Christian and yet not dependent on the metaphors of first century Christianity. But perhaps the quality most important and most difficult to communicate to present day Christians is this one: It will be available here and it will be available now.

My first clear glimpse of this spirituality was in the life and teachings of one Jesus of Nazereth, so it is fitting that we begin with Him.

We could tell the story this way.

Jesus came into history among the Jews. They had been waiting for a Messiah. Although there were a few who had a much more profound understanding of this Messiah, for the masses the expectation took this form: This Messiah was expected to make things much better. Life was pretty miserable for them, but when the Messiah arrived life would be wonderful. All of us at one time or another have been caught expecting some kind of messiah, so we can easily identify with the situation. When my ship comes in, when I graduate from college, when I get my promotion, when I get married...at that time life will take on the abundant quality for which we all hope. Jesus attacked that illusionary variety of the Messiah expectation head-on. He declared that the "kingdom" that was to be inaugurated by the Messiah was already present. It was "at hand", was "in their midst", it was "within them." Some identified Jesus himself as the Messiah. That was even more of an affront. Jesus was changing nothing. The Romans were still in charge. Poverty was still rampant. Sickness and disease were still the order of the day. This was definitely not the Messiah that they were expecting. And the kingdom that he announced was not the kingdom that people had been taught to expect. He was quickly eliminated from the scene.

Yet in another sense, Jesus was extremely good news. Many years ago I was waiting at a bus stop in San Francisco. I waited quite some time before someone came by and informed me that the bus did not come by that stop on that particular day. That was the bad news that was at the same time good news. I was suddenly able to deal with the real situation. Without that good news, I might still be waiting there. So with many of the people who heard Jesus. They were delighted to finally hear that the actual situation of their lives could be embraced. That they did not have to wait for a better deal. Is it not obvious when it is stated? One either lives one's life as it is given, or one does not live. What alternative is there? Only illusion. Such was the "Gospel" that Jesus introduced into the world. God is in the midst of our actual lives making them whole and holy. Given that fact, should we ask whether this is all there is? If we do, the bad news which is good news is that indeed yes, this is all there is. Let us rejoice and be glad. This must have been the Messiah!

Meanwhile over in the Hellenistic world, the cosmology was of a different hue. Over there people believed in the two-story universe that we have described. They believed that this world is manifestly NOT the kingdom of God. They believed it to be a poor imitation of the more perfect world to come. Everything good and holy was located in the second story. As I was working on these pages, I had a familiar experience. I was in a hospital with a family whose beautiful, gifted daughter had just died at the age of twenty. A good friend and minister said to the family: "This life is a nightmare...we can only hope that one day we wake up in heaven." I cringed. I knew that this young girl's life had been a thing of rich blessing and beauty...not by any stretch had it been a nightmare. Such is the continuing presence of the platonic view of life.

Certainly it must have seemed a difficult task getting the Gospel of Jesus adapted to fit that different cosmos. Yet it had to be done. Any religion that did not deal with the problem of getting people out of the imperfect world and into the perfect world would simply not fly. Christianity was made to fit the mold. It began to teach that this world was a fallen and depraved place and that the next world was our real home. Of course it would be inappropriate for us to stand in the midst of our cosmology and pass judgement on people for how they related to their own cosmology. Their cosmology was the real world for them. They did the best they could.

However that may be, the good news for us is that the cosmology in which we presently live is very well-suited for Jesus' original message. Our universe does not have any second floor, it has no dualism, it has no perfect and imperfect realms. Our cosmology tells us very clearly that the life we have is it. Is this all there is? Hundreds of billions of galaxies and seventeen billion years of history is what there is and it is wonderfully adequate. And at the same time it is far more than we can grasp. Its wonder always exceeds our grasp and that makes it open-ended. It is all there is, but there is more to it than I can ever completely grasp. Each day might include a new revelation of wonder. Jesus seems to have grasped the wonder of it quite adequately.

The best place to look for Jesus' understanding of the Kingdom is among his parables. The Kingdom, he says, is like a farmer who plants seed and then is amazed to see them growing and producing. They grow, the parable says, "He knows not how." The Kingdom appears among us quite apart from our own effort or our own belief system. We happen to see a touch of beauty and we say "Ah." It is the Kingdom in our midst.

The Kingdom, he says, is like a man who found a treasure in a field and immediately went and sold everything he had in order to buy the field. When the glory of life appears among us, and we become aware of it, we turn and give it our full devotion. It is like the movie, "Grand Canyon." A man saw the Canyon and was forever transformed. He saw a depth of glory in the midst of life that kept him quite alive even in the midst of very inhumane circumstances. Indeed he could not wait to take other people to the Canyon so that they too might experience the Kingdom.

The Kingdom, Jesus says, is like a son who went away from home and lived a less-than-human life. Then when that son came to himself, he returned to his father and his father received him with open arms and a celebrative heart. No matter how distant we might become or how out of touch with the sacred Center we might be, we can at any time in any place turn back and be warmly received. It is an unconditional gift. The rain falls on the just and the unjust. Here and now is a cosmic "Graceland" where we have "reason to believe we will all be received"...as Paul Simon sings so nicely in his song.

It is my belief that Jesus revealed his theology of salvation to us in that parable of the prodigal son. Nowhere in the authentic sayings of Jesus do we find that business of a Father sending his Son to be sacrificed for the sins of all humankind. Here in this parable is the simple way to the Sacred Center: Simply turn away from illusionary living, open your eyes and it is there. Its arms are open and its message is acceptance. Wherever you are is home.

Other parables give us additional insight. This Kingdom comes upon us unexpectedly. "Like a thief in the night." We are to always be ready for receive the "Bridegroom." We should have oil in our lamps. We should be awake. We don't want to ever pass by the color purple and not notice it, as Shug warned us so eloquently in *The Color Purple*.

On that long ago day when I came upon the cow giving birth to her calf in the pasture, I could have just passed by. I could have been so occupied with some errand that I would have not noticed. Oh, I tremble to think of it. How much poorer my life would have been. The bridegroom came and I was awake and I had oil in my lamp and I was blessed. I did not know anything at all about Jesus' admonitions on this subject. What I did know was very separated from what I experienced that day. No matter. I was awake and I was blessed. Since that day there has been an awareness in me that I should be awake and alert to the glories of life.

Just recently I looked out my back window and saw our huge azalea bush in full bloom. It was two shades of pink along with lots of white. It was covered with all of that beauty. It was utterly overwhelming. I could imagine myself doing everything I possibly could do in order to be able to see that beauty again. At that moment, I could not imagine myself wondering if that was all the blessing I was going to get.

I suppose all of us want to have "abundant life." We want to live life to the full and it may be that we want to be fully in touch with "God." In our recent history, though, it seems to me that we have seldom had that privilege. Rather, we have projected real abundant, communion-with-God living into the past and into the future. We have claimed great things for our ancient forebears. Abraham and Isaac and Jacob and Paul and Silas all had very real and very life-transforming experiences with God. They were in touch with the Sacred Center. They even had literal conversations with God. Oh yes. They had it all. They had the abundant life that Jesus talked about. They could call on God almost any time and get a miracle accomplished. Oh my! But we don't have that privilege. We don't live in biblical days. And we claim great things for ourselves after we die. On that day we shall know everything, understand everything, have total and perfect communion with God. But not now. So we live out our lives being told by the church that both past and future are blessed times, but that the "here and now" is not.

The new spirituality of which I speak is a call to the here and now. It is a celebration of the here and now. It is a proclamation of the divinity of every moment. Here and now!

There is another facet of this that I don't want us to miss. This spirituality is available to everyone. It is here and now for everyone.

This spirituality of which I speak is exoteric rather than esoteric. It is not dependent on the mastery of any special skills of meditation or concentration. Indeed, I have always been a failure at such practices. Yet, I believe I am a spiritual person.

Indeed, I have wondered about the types of meditative practices which stress a kind of "looking past" the normal things of this world in order to experience a kind of spiritual ecstasy or victory. I know that there are devotees of certain spiritualities who spend literally years developing the skill to move into a different state of being. I wonder if that fits well with a cosmos which is so thoroughly our home as this one is. It may be that it comes from an earlier cosmology which stressed escape from this life. Of course, this world is so thoroughly mysterious that I am reluctant to deny the possibility of wealth beyond my own capacity to receive. What I do want to stress is that the spirituality of which I speak is thoroughly here and now. It is in the dimension in which we all normally live. No special skills of transcendence need be developed. It is only necessary that we be awake and that we have "oil in our lamps".

THE TRUTH SHALL MAKE YOU FREE

The New Spirituality will be characterized by integrity. It will be wedded to the truth. It will reach out to the real and hallow it, regardless of what that real may be.

It is a severe contradiction to have a spirituality which fears the truth and constantly seeks to do battle against it. I was riding on a bus in Taiwan and a young Chinese student sat down beside me. He was fairly fluent in English and he wanted to practice. In the town where I lived, there were not many foreigners and so assertive Chinese students were always seeking out an American with whom they might practice. This student was interested in our religion. He could not understand, he said, how any educated person could believe that a body could be dead for three days and then come alive again. The truth is that such a thing did not happen. This is not to deny that "God can do anything He (sic) wants to do." It is simply to say that God did not bring a body back to life after three days. It is inconceivable according to all the truth that we know about this universe. It is also irrational. It makes no sense in this real world. As a metaphor about how new life comes out of deadness, it is in fact powerful. As a description of a real event, it is a denial of the real. It therefore is actually destructive of the message of the gospel: "Life is good and can be embraced." The "life" that is good is the life in which dead bodies do not come alive after three days of decay. Surely we have seen this deep contradiction in our story for a long time. Why have we neglected to clarify the issue? The answer we all know: Our spirituality has been insecure in the face of truth.

No spirituality can have power in the lives of people if that spirituality fears the truth. The goal of a vital spirituality is to help people relate in a healthy way to the environment in which they live. We live in the cosmos. We live in the midst of reality. We need a spirituality which fearlessly embraces the real. A spirituality which does less will be of no help. A spirituality which does less may very well be demonic. The "demons" of any age are those forces which seek to have us deny the goodness of the creation and which seek to have us say "no" rather than "yes" to the reality of our own existence.

Imagine it: A spirituality which celebrates the work of the scientists. Every new discovery is applauded and its mysteries fully exploited for the experience of awe. Every new discovery is an occasion to alter our behavior towards a more valid relationship with reality. Imagine a spirituality that celebrates the work of the artists. Every new creation from the artist is an occasion for celebration. Rather than fearing that the artist might cross some boundary of "morality", we will rejoice even when we are staggered. This one touched a spot of pain in us. What does that say about us? What are we hiding from anyway? We are eager, always, to have our eyes opened more fully to the deeps of life.

No, this does not mean that we will be naive or gullible. Quite the opposite. Being set free from loyalty to misunderstandings of the past, we will be able to more easily evaluate new discoveries with a clear head. Recently a religious publication crossed my desk which contained an extensive article defending "creationism" against evolution. It was a tired old argument, but it was done in a scholarly fashion. What was evident, however, was that the author was struggling to defend an old explanation of the way things are. Set him free from that need and he will be a new man. The way things actually *are* is what we are to love. The way our religion has *told* us things are, is...by comparison...of much lesser importance. That God created the real, we can be sure. That God created the religious dogma, we can never be sure. The REAL will set us free. And we shall be free indeed. (John 8:32 & 36)

The new spirituality will be deeply in love with the "way it is", and will trust it to always be a blessing. It is, after all, the place where we meet the Holy. There is no other place. This also means that the new spirituality will be faithful to the central message of Jesus: "The Kingdom is at hand!"

The new spirituality, therefore, will immerse itself in the cosmos. This is actually a re-statement of the above, but is stated separately because of our record of distancing ourselves from the cosmos.

I am tempted to use the word "nature", but have chosen the word "cosmos" because it is a more inclusive word. When I say the cosmos I mean the whole thing, the entire universe. The new spirituality will be nourished most of all by the Mystery in the midst of the cosmos. The centuries-long chasm between the human ones and the cosmos will be ended. Humanity will have permission to embrace the obvious: The cosmos itself is the dwelling place of God. We encounter the Mystery in the galaxies. We encounter the Mystery in the planets. We encounter the Mystery in the Moon. We encounter the Mystery in the earth in all of its glory. The mountains fill us with awe. The rivers fill us with awe. The sea fills us with awe. The animals, the birds, the flowers, the trees, the whales, the fish...they all fill us with a deep sense of the Mystery. We encounter God in them all. No, this is not pantheism. Those glorious gifts are not God. We encounter God *in* them (panentheism). Since God is, in our tradition, honored as Creator; what more likely place would there be to find God? But I am not convinced of this because it makes sense. I am convinced of this because in my own life I have found it to be so. I have come to be close to the Mystery by falling in love with the cosmos. I fell in love with the cosmos because I discovered that the cosmos was hopelessly in love with me. Fifty years ago I paddled out onto the majestic Santee river in South Carolina and instantly I knew that I had found a friend. I could not begin to say how many times I have been blessed by that river. The river itself blesses me. The sense of awe that the river occasions in me from time to time blesses me even more. Such has been my life-long experience with the cosmos in which we live.

A spirituality that thrives off the wonder of the cosmos! What a marvelous thing. There is no end to the ecstasy. There is no end to the surprise. There is no end to the Mystery. There is no end to the variety. The splendor of the cosmos is indeed eternal. This spirituality will have an endless supply of energy. It will never be boring.

It is abundantly clear to all the earth that we need such a spirituality. We need a spirituality that reunites us with nature. Enough of the kind of insecure spirituality which teaches human superiority. We need a spirituality that teaches unity with nature. We are all one. In very truth, we have proven false any claim to superiority over other creatures. What other creature has done damage to the planet equal to what we have done? This spring as I spaded up my garden I uncovered a large healthy earthworm. It occurred to me how superior to me that worm was in the task of caring for the planet. This worm spends its entire life making the soil richer. As far as I can tell it does nothing at all except bring benefit to the planet. What do I do that is equally beneficial? In fact, it is quite probable that as a result of my life the planet will be less healthy...in spite of my efforts to make a positive contribution. Forget superiority! Let us hope for equality! Let us cherish the notion that we are all equal. That is not a rational conclusion. That is experiential. Get close to the cosmos. Let go of a few of your control mechanisms, and it will happen to you. You will experience unity with all that is. That, I believe, is the central religious experience. If a person claims to love God but does not love the creation, that person is a liar. (See I John 4:20) That experience of unity with God as God is encountered in the actual world is the wellspring from which genuine spirituality emerges.

And guess what else? We are included. The cosmos includes me. I fall in love with the cosmos and in the process I am falling in love with my own existence. Let's be done with the old "hatred of the flesh" spirituality! We need a spirituality which celebrates our very human-ness. Our human "nature" is intimately interwoven with all of nature. A countless variety of little organisms live in our bodies, helping us to live. We would die without them. A countless variety of organisms give up their lives each day so that we can live. We would die without them. Our backbones were invented by the fish. Our arms were developed by the primates. We are all one. It is all one glorious web of beauty and interdependence. Our bodies are good. Our sensualities and appetites are good. It is all a marvelous gift. The new spirituality will invite us to celebrate and hold sacred the depths and heights of our humanity.

61

The cosmos is the well in which the living water is found. Any little facet of it can at any time serve as a window through which we see the Mystery (God). For that reason, we will learn to hold sacred every thing that is. Both rattlesnakes and new born babies are valued. Heterosexuals and homosexuals are equally valued. Men and women, dark and light, plant and animal, friend and foe...all are valued. We are all filled with Mystery. We are each one of us a blessing to the rest of us.

So the "Great Separation" is ended. The effort to deny the twentieth century is finally over. The effort to hide in ancient metaphors is over. The effort by the branch of the primate family called human to separate itself from the rest of the creation is over. We now find our eternal significance in the midst of the actual world in which we live. Finally we agree with the first chapter of Genesis: "It is very good." We have embraced the truth and the truth has set us free.

Well, perhaps that is to overstate the case. We are **struggling** at long last to embrace the truth, to be at home in the cosmos into which we have been born. In some ways it is a strange new world for those of us who have been in the religious sphere for a while. As the pioneers pushed their way into the western part of what is now the United States, they always hired "scouts" from among the Native Americans to lead them. They needed someone who knew the territory. They needed the wisdom of people who had lived in the land for a while. So it is with us. We should not expect professional religious people to be very adept at navigating the land of Mystery after a lifetime of pretending it did not exist. Therefore we should be very glad to obtain the help of some "scouts." And yes, there are such scouts available.

Indeed, if we were able to stand at some distance, there are a few things which would surely amaze us: There has been a community of human beings...the scientists...for several centuries now who have been radically committed to the truth. They have been committed to following it wherever it might lead. That is amazing. They were not especially religious people. In fact, for the sake of their work, they set religion to the side. They did not let it interfere with their work, so to speak. That is amazing. That the religion of the day would not be vitally involved in the search for the truth is amazing. That the religion of the day could be easily set aside from the search is also amazing. Even more amazing is the fact that the organized religion of the day actually looked at the search for truth with some misgivings. In some cases, the religious structures vigorously opposed the search for truth. What kind of religion is this? But how wonderful that the search for truth continued.

We should not, however, be overly harsh in our judgement of the church from our perch in the late twentieth century. In the midst of the Cartesian/Newtonian era things looked different. On the one hand, we were convinced that there were laws in the universe that were absolutely fixed in place. The church could be excused for assuming that its dogma was included. At the same time, the search for truth seemed to undermine some of that dogma. What to do? We tried simply putting the scientific enterprise aside as irrelevant to the religious sphere. When that did not work, we opposed the scientists as agents of the devil. A few brave souls tried to integrate the truth into the belief system of the church. As we have seen, they were not exactly praised for their work. The insights of most were confined to the ivory towers of seminary. Some were persecuted, and any pastor today who speaks forthrightly on this matter will probably feel the ground tremble beneath his pulpit.

We should also acknowledge here that the scientists were not blameless during this time. They were going through what might be called the adolescent phase of science. They "knew everything", or thought they soon might. Life was not at the center mysterious. It was simply a machine to be figured out. Such an attitude is understandable, given the times. However, it is also understandable that religious folk would be threatened. Where is their realm? Where might be their livelihood?

There is, however, at the center of this issue a "pearl of great price": The willingness to follow the truth no matter where it might lead. This is not just a foundation stone for the scientific establishment, it is also a foundation stone for any relevant and effective spirituality. I find myself amazed at the capacity of the scientist to abandon, for instance, an hypothesis that s/he has worked on for half a lifetime because it has been proven inaccurate by new evidence. I have tried to imagine what it must have been like for scientists schooled thoroughly in the Newtonian system of thought to be confronted by the Einstein articles published in 1905. What must it have been like for Einstein himself? How many sleepless nights? How much agonizing self-doubt? Yet it is precisely that kind of struggle that lies at the heart of spiritual growth. How do I enlarge my little world to include a new portion of the "real" world outside my own little self-serving system. How do I let the truth bring destruction to my illusion? How do I give up the comfort of my neat little religious system for the sake of a larger, more uncertain world? This is the place where religion and science should find common ground. At the present moment in history, the religious community needs to sit at the feet of the scientific community for a while. (It should be noted, however, that scientists are fallible like the rest of us and sometimes sell their souls for a morsel of bread.)

Here is another gift the scientists give us. They reveal the wonder of the universe to us. They surprise us with awesome bits of information. They tell us that there are maybe a trillion galaxies out there. A trillion! Wow! Our minds are unable to grasp it. We are staggered! They tell us that this little caterpillar has the capacity to inflate itself with air so that it is much larger than its normal size and so that its rear end will look like the head of a snake. How could such an invention happen? We hear all the various explanations for it and still we are blown away! I subscribe to *National Geographic* and to *Discover* primarily for the purpose for getting some new "awesome" piece of data. It feeds my soul. How sad that the Christian community, as a rule, has deprived itself of this wonderful information. How sad that we would take a little piece of ancient poetry (Genesis 1) and try to impose that poetry in a literal fashion on the science of the world. That one little tragedy reveals much about our intellectual waywardness and our insecurity, but it reveals much more: It reveals our inability to be richly blessed by the depth and splendor of the universe. That is tragic beyond words.

The greatest gift, then, that we have received from the scientific community needs to be clearly stated: They have led us back into the realm of Mystery. They have ushered the twentieth century back into the awareness of the unknown. As I have pointed out (See Chapter Two) the Einsteinian revolution has taken us right up to the edge of Mystery and has invited us to leap into it. It is clear now that Mystery is the order of the day. No, not because that is a good idea, but because that is simply the way it is. I cannot begin to express my appreciation for the many ways in which the work of the scientists of the twentieth century has blessed my life. I am rich with wonder.

We now enter a new time...a time when the human family will be creating a new spirituality. We hope now to have an end to the conflict of past years. We hope the practitioners of religion will be of some help in constructing the new spirituality. We hope they will be able to turn loose their old assumptions in much the same way that scientists were able to do following Einstein's 1905 bombshell. A vision of religious functionaries with such courage indeed tests one's credulity, but hope we must. Whether or not such a miracle does occur, I am sure of one thing: The scientists will play the larger role. They, after all, are already trained in following the truth with a relentless obedience. I have also seen signs of such depth of spirit among some of the poet/scientists (Annie Dillard, Brian Swimme, Fritjof Capra) of our day that I am extremely proud to have them leading the way toward a spirituality rooted in reality. They are our heroes.

There are two favors I would like to ask of the scientific community: First, I beg them to abandon the old "hands off" attitude toward religion. My friends, we need you to hold our feet to the fire. We need you to say to us, "That is several hundred years out of date!" or "That is simply not true!." Your silence has not helped us much. It has probably contributed to our luxurious irrelevance. We can only wonder what might have happened if the scientific community had kept itself involved in the religious enterprise through these recent centuries and had required of the church the same level of honesty that is taken for granted among scientists. I call this request a favor because I could certainly understand it if the scientific community looked on such a request with some disdain and with no sense of obligation. After all, the church has not been much of a friend to science over these years.

My second request is this: Please don't patronize us. Don't do little quasi-scientific programs to support us in our illusions. Let's have no Christmas programs at the local observatory which purport to show how there is a scientific basis for the star that the wise men saw. Simply acknowledge that the story is myth. There were no wise men. There was no star. It is Matthew's attempt to communicate in story form the universality of the gospel message. It is a beautiful story. It is horrendous as factual data. We do not believe in astrology. It is impossible for a star to move ahead of people and stop over a stable in Bethlehem. We know that you know better. Let's have no "expeditions" searching for Noah's ark. Let's forget the

64

"scientific" investigation of the Shroud of Turin. It is all a confusion of story with fact. We have been able to confuse that issue quite well on our own. We need you to simply tell us the truth. We want to be able to count on that.

Finally, it should be clear that in the twentieth century everyone is a scientist. Actually, the truth is more radical: Everyone is the milky way, everyone is the sun, everyone is the little bird building its nest. It is all one thing. This book is just as much a creation of the galaxy as it is my own creation. Everything is vitally inter-related. No longer can there be a "religious" realm and a "scientific" realm. I think the galaxies had a meeting and decided that such an illusion could not be allowed in the universe any longer. And who are we to argue with several hundred billion galaxies! So let us all follow the truth with confidence. Let us all bathe in the radiance of each new insight. Let us all be blown away by the awe-full Mystery that is hidden in every blade of grass. After all, the cosmos is our friend. The only truth that exists is contained in the deep recesses of the cosmos. When we cut ourselves off from that truth, we are cut off indeed.

SOLIDARITY IS THE NEW NAME FOR LOVE

It was in 1988 in the little village of El Corral in a Contra-infested part of Nicaragua that it became most clear to me. The priest in that village was very active in trying to improve the lives of those poverty-stricken and war-ravaged people. He had been helping them on a water project which was one reason that our Witness for Peace delegation was there. They were putting a water line from up in the mountains down to the village so that everyone could have pure water to drink. The problem was the Contra. They were in the mountains and that made it very dangerous for villagers to venture there to work on the water line. We were there to "accompany" the villagers up into the mountains to complete the work. On this particular afternoon we were sitting in a circle in the little church having a conversation with the village priest. He was a native of Colombia. He served the indigenous people there for many years, but following a massacre by government forces he had been so outspoken as to become persona non grata in Colombia. He then volunteered to serve in El Corral. He was also a Franciscan. We asked him about his relationship with North American Franciscans. They tended to serve the people in the old way, he said. He tended to work in the new way. The old way is the way of charity. The new way is the way of building community structures of justice and health. The church in Latin America was, even as he spoke, painfully divided along that continental divide. What I saw that day in El Corral was this: The church has traditionally substituted charity for justice. The people of Latin America were in the midst of trying a new way.

Pope John the Twenty-third is quoted as having said, "There is no charity without justice." That spirit pervaded the church in the early years following the Vatican Council and out of that spirit the "Popular Church" movement and "Liberation Theology" were born. Traditionally, of course, the church in Latin

America (as in North America) has been allied with the powerful and rich. The church was quite willing to take offerings and collect clothing for the poor majority. It was a happy arrangement: The church enjoyed all the advantages of the elite and salved its conscience by providing morsels of food to the poor who were made poor by the oppressive policies of the elite. It is an extreme scenario in the third world, but it is very typical of the Christian church almost anywhere you find it. The Popular Church grew by leaps and bounds across Latin America in those early years. In Nicaragua it supported the Sandinista movement quite openly. After all, there was little choice for the poor. Should they have allied themselves with Samoza? The hierarchy of the Nicaraguan church continued to follow the old way. Indeed, the Cardinal in Managua never even went so far as to speak out against the atrocities being committed as a strategy of war by the Contra forces. The division was very clear.

We wonder how this came about. How could a religion based on the Hebrew Prophets and the Prophet of Galilee so easily be used as a support system for injustice?

To put the matter in bold relief: Imagine a society where the richest and most powerful people own almost all of the economic resources. Give that small portion of the population control of almost all of the means of communication. Give that small group, in addition, a system where they can have enormous influence on who gets elected and on how they vote, once elected. Then, as if that were not enough, add a religious system that also easily supports the whims of the elite and even pours holy water over their sins.. This is a system designed to benefit the wealthy and oppress the poor. Such is the system we have in the United States as well as in Latin America.

Add to this the theology of escape. Life on this earth is not really important anyway. The only life that matters is in the next world. The church is concerned about the "spiritual realm" which is primarily other-worldly. It matters little how much you hurt people in this life so long as you care about their "spiritual" well-being. To be over-concerned with justice is to betray a dangerous tendency toward "this-world-ness." It does not miss the attention of the oppressed, however, that the oppressors seem quite interested in the accouterments of this world.

Colonialism gave us an example of how easily this pliable religion could be molded into a friendly relationship with the most extreme practices of cruelty. Columbus is said to have hanged twelve indigenous men at a time to symbolize the twelve disciples. Their crime? They did not bring the required amount of gold to him on schedule. The song "Amazing Grace" is said to have been composed on a slave ship as it carried its suffering cargo across the Atlantic. John Bowring looked across the "wrecks of time" and saw a church steeple with a cross on it. It inspired him to write "In the Cross of Christ I Glory." The "wrecks of time" in fact were on the Chinese coast having just been bombarded by "Christian" forces imposing the opium trade on a reluctant Chinese government. The story is not pretty. The "Great Separation" is stark against the skyline...more visible by far than that cross on the

66

steeple.

Some historians suggest that the tragic turn took place in the fourth century with the decision of Constantine to make Christianity the state religion. Certainly that did not bode well for a religion that was born amidst the poor and powerless. We are hard-pressed to find post-Constantine examples of the religious hierarchy coming down on the side of the poor and oppressed, though there are countless examples of individuals and small groups doing so. The Popular Church in Latin America is all the more remarkable for the contrast.

Suppose, then, that we were going to have a spirituality that does not promote injustice, but which has justice at the very center. To begin discussing such a spirituality, I return to Nicaragua. The year was 1994. The Contra war was history. The economic devastation of the war years was now capped by a peacetime economic policy designed to improve the national economy on the backs of the poor. These so-called "structural adjustment policies" by now had driven Nicaragua down into Haiti's economic neighborhood. We sat in a room and heard the devastation discussed at length. Then the speaker said these words, "Solidarity is the new name for love." He was suggesting that the only way we can love Nicaragua is to be "with" her in the deepest and most spiritual sense. In that statement is found the relationship of the new spirituality to justice.

This new spirituality begins with the experience of awe. As Abraham Heschel put it, "Awe precedes faith." Let me go back to my experience of seeing the cow give birth to her calf. I experienced awe. But that experience of awe is not empty. It is rich with content. I experienced unity. I experienced care. I could not have been unconcerned about that little calf's well-being. I had been wedded to it. Justice is born in the experience of wonder-filled unity with all that is. Eastern religions have been aware of this for a long time. The religious experience is an experience of unity. Let me give a few illustrations:

The first time I walked into the Grand Canyon and every time since I have been awe-struck. I fall in love with life, with my own existence, with the cosmos, every time I walk those trails. I find myself caring. Automatically, I find myself caring. I care about the Canyon. I feel some anger when an airplane flies too close. I bristle when I hear that some James Watt wants to turn it into a Disneyland. I care. The care is born at the moment of awe. The awe binds me to the creation. We are all one.

In 1991 I was in Bluefields, Nicaragua. Bluefields is on the Atlantic coast and was devastated by the Contra War. It was then devastated by Hurricane Joan. It was then devastated by the post-war economic debacle. Unemployment stood at 85%. One afternoon I was on the back of a truck as we toured the worst poverty I had ever seen. Children were playing in mud. Women were standing knee deep in a very polluted stream washing clothes. Houses were little more than carefully arranged collections of scraps. It was a very depressing ride. We gringos were taking pictures of this misery to use later in the influencing of public opinion in the United States. The noble purpose did not adequately silence our internal protests at the indignity

67

of it. Then we turned a corner and I saw a little girl dressed in a very clean yellow dress sitting beside the road. She looked like she was about to attend a party. She was a touch of beauty in a very bleak picture. She was a rose growing out of rocks. We passed by and I know I will never see her again, but her presence is burned into my consciousness. In the moment that I saw her I knew that she and I were family. She was my sister, my daughter, my own flesh. It was an incredible experience of unity. Nothing can happen to her or to her country and it not matter to me. Justice flows naturally out of the experience of unity. It is powered by the sense of awe.

The new spirituality has this wonderful gift: Justice is at the very center of it. In the first place, it is purely experiential. You experience the holy Mystery of this cosmos and you care about the well being of all the creation.

In the second place justice is at the very center of the new cosmology and of the new physics. One of the fundamental premises of the Einsteinian view of reality is that it is all inter-related. All of it is important to all the rest of it. Our experience fits very nicely with the truth as our best physicists have been able to discern it. When a leaf falls in my back yard, it makes a difference in the furthest galaxy. It is all inter-related in infinite ways. We could use the word love to describe it. Love is built into the universe. Everything cares about everything else at the most basic levels. A better word is the word compassion. Matthew Fox wrote a book on compassion some years ago which illuminated this for me.[*] Compassion is the experience of unity. "Sympathy", on the other hand, is the experience of separateness, of superiority. Sympathy says "I want to help you, you poor unfortunate soul." Compassion says "You and I are one."

In the third place, the new spirituality will return us to the biblical view that we are all the same. We are all equally children of God. We are all equally valuable. The Hebrew prophets were revolutionary in their insight at this point. They saw that poor people were just as valuable as rich people. They did not know twentieth century physics, but they knew their own experience. They experienced the unity, the "ties that bind us", and they were transformed by that experience. It was the prophets of the eighth century B.C. who gave me my best instruction in justice in the early years of seminary and ministry. A few months ago I stood at the Civil Rights Memorial in Montgomery, Alabama and put my hand in the water to touch the names of the martyrs of the Civil Rights Movement. As I felt the cool waters running over my fingers, I looked up and saw Amos' words, "Let justice roll down like waters and righteousness like an ever-flowing stream." Amos and Dr. Martin Luther King Jr., who quoted him so eloquently, knew that we are all one. That reality powered the revolution toward equality in our land. It is at the root of all work for justice. Justice that does not begin with that sense of unity tends to burn itself out very quickly.

---

[*] Fox, Matthew. *A Spirituality Named Compassion.* Minneapolis: Winston Press, 1979.

Jesus also preached a justice that is founded in the unity of us all. He suggested that we treat the very least as we would treat him (Matthew 25:40). Not because it was a good thing or even because He insisted on it, but because the very least ARE Jesus. We are all one. It is also clear that the early church, with its roots still in the homes of the oppressed, understood justice to be at the center of its spirituality. How else might we explain the Magnificat's (Luke 1:51 & 52) suggestion that God is active in putting down the mighty from their thrones and scattering the proud while exalting those of low degree? There is at the Holy Center a force which seeks to honor all people regardless of circumstance.

I believe it was the church's expansion into the "alien" cosmology of the Hellenistic world that weakened its commitment to Justice. The alienation was thorough enough to make it a taken-for-granted truth that oppressors through the ages have very often used the Christian religion to make their oppression more palatable to the oppressed. There will be "pie in the sky by and by." Most recently the Reagan administration actively encouraged the expansion of fundamentalist Protestantism in Latin America as a way to defuse the power of Liberation Theology. Fundamentalist preachers were enlisted to preach to the Contra troops.

Nevertheless, there have been giants throughout history who were so in touch with the Holy Center that their commitment to justice powered their lives. They transcended the dualistic teachings of the majority and bathed their souls in the Biblical message of justice. I remember talking to a young woman in El Salvador who had spent fourteen years in the struggle for justice in that tortured land. She told me that all of her colleagues of her own age group who had gone into the struggle with her were dead. They were all dead except her. She alone had survived to see the possibility, however fragile, of peace. Someone asked her what happened to her at the age of fourteen that sent her into the struggle. She said it happened while she was studying the Bible. So it has happened for the "Prophetic Remnant" throughout history. In spite of all the barriers and all of the unselfconscious church's pablum, these people break through.

I dream now of a new day. A day when the new spirituality will make available to a larger number of people a sense of justice that is powered by their own experience, by their own understanding of the cosmos in which we live, and by the witness of the Bible. Of course, there will always be a majority who are blinded to the Holy in our midst, but surely we can do better than we have done in recent centuries.

THE CENTRALITY OF STORY

There is an old joke about three umpires. One is a fundamentalist, one is a liberal and one is an existentialist. The fundamentalist says "I call 'em like they are." The liberal says "I call 'em like I see 'em." The existentialist umpire says "They ain't nothing 'til I call 'em." That third position is actually our situation as human beings on planet earth in the late twentieth century. Reality is not anything, as far as our actual living is concerned, until we say what reality is. There is no "objective" reality out there apart from our effort to observe it and report on it. No one ever sees "actual" reality. They only have their observation of it, which physicists tell us actually is different depending on the observer and on the moment of observation. Indeed, all we have is the story. Never has it been so clear that the story is vital to our existence.

There is also the Old Testament wisdom that "No one ever sees the face of God and lives." Another way to state that is to say that there are no living humans who have seen the Mystery as it actually is. For instance, the actual "stuff" that makes up the city of Greenville is almost non-existent. Perhaps all together it would amount to the head of a pin. The whirling atoms and conglomerates of molecules are almost all empty space. That space is filled with waves of energy and forces of inter-relatedness, but the actual sub-atomic particles all together would amount to almost nothing at all. Indeed sometimes those particles are not particles at all, but are waves. What they are at any moment depends on the observer and on the moment of observation. Obviously if we could actually see reality clearly, we would not be able to function at all. How would we find the supermarket if all we could see was empty space.

To add to the mix there is this: The description I just wrote of reality is also a story. It is not reality. We do not know what reality is. It is a fairly accurate description of reality as best we can imagine it at this moment. A few hundred years from now the best description of it might be as different as our current story is different from the Newtonian story.

It is essential that we have a story (a picture, a mask) which enables us to function in the reality of our own time. The story is all we have. We relate to the story, for the most part, as if it were reality. The story, in turn, must be as closely related to reality as is possible in the given moment. Otherwise the story might lead us badly astray. Imagine the astronauts taking off for the moon with a pre-Copernican story. Imagine trying to cure depression with a demonology story. It is, obviously, a perpetual task. We get a bit of new information concerning the cosmos and we create a new story. We get a bit more information and we revise our story. Later the new information is so radically different that we have to toss out one story and build another. That is the best that we can do.

There does seem to be one new element in our present story. Our present story tells us that the story is always imperfect. I believe it is true that in all previous ages the story claimed perfection for itself. People tended to say, this is THE story rather than A story. However, we are yet to be really tested. How will we respond when it becomes clear that Einstein missed the mark as much as Newton? And, of course, in many areas of our lives, we are hanging onto stories which are long since inadequate. A row of tobacco industry officials sat before Congress and swore that tobacco was not addictive. Fundamentalist Christians swear that the Biblical creation story is literally accurate. Alcoholics across the planet are swearing by the story of their self-control. Sometimes reality has to use a two-by-four to get our

70

attention.

Why am I not more successful in my profession? I have a story for that. The story has changed a little in recent years, but I have a story. It helps me feel OK about myself. The story I tell myself may not be very accurate. Probably other people could help me improve it...if I were to be honest enough to tell them that such things matter to me. Sometimes people tell a story about such matters which sends them into the Post Office with an assault weapon. It is helpful if our story is fairly closely related to the truth, but of this we can be sure: It will never BE the truth, because no one sees that and lives. One might try imagining for a moment how many books it would take to tell such a story if every element of the story was included.

Why did Philadelphia sweep the Braves in a four game series in Atlanta? Everyone who cares at all about such things has a story which may not be anywhere close to reality, but which enables that person to continue to...or refuse to... pay twenty bucks for a ticket.

As I write these words we are trying in this country to build a coherent story which would help us to understand why a building in Oklahoma City was blown up. From the first moment we have been building stories and revising them and throwing them out and starting over. The truth, of course, we will never know. But we must have a story which will enable us to deal responsibly with the situation and make responsible decisions about the future. It will help a lot if the story if fairly accurate.

It is very difficult for us to acknowledge the demise of a story which has been very dear to our hearts. Not many were pleased to hear that the earth was not the center of the universe. I can remember the anger with which many people received the news that the Old Testament passage (quoted in the New Testament) which was supposed to say "virgin" actually said "young woman." Just a tiny part of a sacred story is touched by reality and the whole house trembles.

I have spent considerable time in earlier chapters spelling out the devastating results of the church's failure to change its story to fit the changing cosmology of the centuries. Most simply put, the story doesn't "work" any more. This is the test of a story: Does it WORK? Does it relate us in a healthy and life-giving way to the actual situation as we know it? Another way to put it is this: "Does it mesh with other current and accepted stories of the culture in such a way as to enable people to live successfully?"

There is a great deal of variety in our stories, in the complexity of them and in the importance of them. I went fishing with my father many times. If the wind was blowing from the east, he would remember a little tiny story: "Wind from the east, fish bite least." That is a little story which seemed to be fairly accurate. Especially it seemed accurate after we noticed the wind and remembered the story. We were not as optimistic or enthusiastic about our fishing after that. In actuality, it is hard for me to conceive that the fish care much about the direction of the wind. Still, though, when I go fishing I would prefer the wind not be blowing from the east.

71

Near the time of my father's death, he asked me if I thought he would go to heaven when he died. Well! Now that is a story of a different hue. That is an immensely important story. It has to do with the significance of one's entire life. It has to do with eternity. In a way it has to do with everything! Stories on this level are usually dignified with the term "myth." We think of mythology as being made up of those stories which are about ultimate matters. Actually, the old divisions are not very relevant any more. It is all story. It is all important. Einstein's E=MC² is a very brief statement of a story, but it is extremely important for our understanding of who we are in century twenty. I am unwilling, therefore, to separate our stories into "sacred" and "profane" categories. That is a problem we are trying to get free of even as we speak. Still I want to suggest that we are in great need of a new mythology. The new spirituality demands a new mythology...new stories which help us relate to the Mystery in a life-giving way.

So we face one of the greater challenges of the human enterprise: the building of a new mythology. It will be an enormous undertaking. It will need to be done in close relationship with the deepest dimensions of our lives. There is surely wisdom hidden in our collective unconscious that can be accessed for this task. We must find ways to do that. We must also use the great untapped creative resources of humankind. We must unleash the "right brain." We must restore creativity to its rightful place as the most "God-like" of all human activities. We must avail ourselves of the wisdom vaults of all cultures and search especially among the remnants of spiritualities which thrived prior to the current "world religions." Those primitive peoples seemed to know something about living in harmony with the universe that we have forgotten. We must get acquainted with the great mystics of the Christian tradition. The work of saints such as Hildegard of Bingen (1098-1179) and Meister Eckhart (1260-1329) promises to be of great worth to us as Matthew Fox has so ably pointed out. This and much more we must do.

At the same time we must avail ourselves of the vast amount of work that has already been done on this task. I believe the most valuable work done in this arena has been done by people who have no great investment in the present religious systems. The scientists, the psychologists, the artists and others have been struggling for some time to break through the barriers of "religiosity" and communicate the truth to us. Let me mention a few illustrations:

Twenty-five years ago when the Ecumenical Institute was leading religious seminars around this country we used a movie which was Rod Sterling's version of *Requiem for a Heavyweight*. It is a wonderful movie. It tells the truth about life. It challenges our sentimentality and shows us a man who experienced new birth and who became a living example of freedom. This movie had as its central focus the communication of the Gospel itself: When your illusion about life is broken and you receive permission to live life as it actually is and you make a decision to say "yes" to that possibility then you are alive indeed. The movie communicates the ancient message very effectively, but it uses no religious language at all. There is no church, no minister, no reference to the Bible, and no traditional Christian symbols. Yet, I

72

dare to suggest, it is a better story for our time than our traditional story of the cross.

Read *Revelation* by Flannery O'Conner.[13] Mrs. Turpin is using religious language to support her rather hilarious illusion about her own status. She, in fact, is in the midst of propping up her illusion with "Jesus" when the truth arrives in the form of a thrown textbook. The book hits her on the head and pretty soon she receives the truth. The story goes on to tell of her vision of her *actual* place in the great scheme of things. One can assume from the ending of the story that Mrs. Turpin was a new woman. She embraced the actual and received new life. The Word of salvation came from a very un-religious source with some very un-religious language. The gospel got communicated in spite of the current religious structures. As I read the story again recently, it occurred to me how very difficult it would have been for Mrs. Turpin to receive salvation in a church service. The church she would likely have attended would have been in support of her illusion. Mrs. Turpin's name is legion. Her story is a life-giving one.

Read a book such as *The Immense Journey* by Loren Eiseley. Whereas the above illustrations are of artists communicating the saving message of the gospel in their work, Eiseley tried to re-connect us with the cosmos by enticing us into its wonder. This, too, is a mode of salvation. When we are re-united with the depth and wonder of the creation, we are saved indeed. I remember especially a section of *The Immense Journey* called "The Snout":

> It began as such things always begin...in the ooze of unnoticed swamps, in the darkness of eclipsed moons. It began with a strangled gasping for air.
>
> The pond was a place of reek and corruption, of fetid smells and of oxygen-starved fish breathing through laboring gills. At times the slowly contracting circle of the water left little windrows of minnows who skittered desperately to escape the sun, but who died, nevertheless, in the fat, warm mud. It was a place of low life. In it the human brain began.
>
> There were strange snouts in those waters, strange barbels nuzzling the bottom ooze, and there was time...three hundred million years of it...but mostly, I think, it was the ooze. By day the temperature in the world outside the pond rose to a frightful intensity; at night the sun went down in smoking red. Dust storms marched in incessant progression across a wilderness whose plants were the plants of long ago. Leafless and weird and stiff they lingered by the water, while over vast areas of grassless uplands the winds blew until red stones took on the polish of reflecting mirrors. There was nothing to hold the land in place. Winds howled, dust clouds rolled, and brief erratic torrents choked with silt ran down to the sea. It was a time of dizzying contrasts, a time of change.

---

[13] Flannery O'Conner, *The Complete Stories* (New York, 1992), p. 488ff.

On the oily surface of the pond, from time to time a snout thrust upward, took in air with a queer grunting inspiration, and swirled back to the bottom. The pond was doomed, the water was foul, and the oxygen almost gone, but the creature would not die. It could breathe air direct through a little accessory lung, and it could walk. In all the weird and lifeless landscape, it was the only thing that could. It walked rarely and under protest, but that was not surprising. The creature was a fish.

In the passage of days the pond became a puddle, but the Snout survived. There was dew one dark night and a coolness in the empty stream bed. When the sun rose next morning the pond was an empty place of cracked mud, but the Snout did not lie there. He had gone. Down stream there were other ponds. He breathed air for a few hours and hobbled slowly along on the stumps of heavy fins.

It was an uncanny business if there had been anyone there to see. It was a journey best not observed in daylight, it was something that needed swamps and shadows and the touch of the night dew. It was a monstrous penetration of a forbidden element, and the Snout kept his face from the light. It was just as well, though the face should not be mocked. In three hundred million years it would be our own.[14]

When I read this story aloud, it always brings tears to my eyes. It is a powerful story about the wonder of the creation. Many other artist-scientists have done similar work.

Likewise the work of Joseph Campbell and others in the realm of mythology will be of great value. Campbell does an excellent job of revealing the universal power of myth in the human journey. He also helps us get some distance on our own particular mythology and see it in a much broader context. When I read *The Power of Myth* I was mesmerized by his insight. I remember especially his comment on the ascension of Jesus. In my own search for meaning amidst the symbols of the Christian Faith I had simply let the ascension go. I could see no redeeming value in it. Campbell said, "For example, Jesus ascended to heaven. The denotation would seem to be that somebody ascended to the sky. That's literally what is being said. But if that were really the meaning of the message, then we have to throw it away, because there would have been no such place for Jesus literally to go. We know that Jesus could not have ascended to heaven because there is no physical heaven anywhere in the universe. Even ascending at the speed of light, Jesus would still be in the galaxy. Astronomy and physics have simply eliminated that as a literal, physical possibility. But if you read 'Jesus ascended to heaven' in terms of its metaphoric connotation, you see that he has gone inward...not into outer space but into inward space, to the place from which all being comes, into the consciousness

---

[14] Loren Eiseley, *The Immense Journey* (New York, 1957), p. 49ff.

that is the source of all things, the kingdom of heaven within."[15] It was a freeing moment for me.

Now we turn to a very exciting aspect of the search for a new mythology. We are actually in the midst of the re-creation of one of our most profound stories. Perhaps at some point in the distant future, when the histories of religions are told, the most important event for the history of religion on planet earth will be this: In the twentieth century a new and universal creation story was born.

Every religion in every culture has its creation story. The story of how the world came into existence and how that event is related to humankind is very important for any people. It informs us about who we are and about the significance of our lives. It also informs us about what our relationship to the rest of the creation should be. The "Creation Story" of a people, at its best, can be a very powerful influence in the affairs of that people.

We, in the Christian tradition, have several creation stories. Our Bible has two of those stories in the first two chapters. The fact that the early editors of the Bible felt comfortable with two quite different creation stories side by side suggests to us that those early folks knew the stories to be metaphorical in nature. As metaphors for the ancient world these stories performed their task quite well. They declared the universe to be the creation of God and humankind to be God's highest accomplishment. The first story also has a very beautiful affirmation of the creation: "And God saw everything that he had made, and behold, it was very good." (Genesis 1:31 RSV) They also supported the patriarchal system of the day and gave permission to the human species to "subdue" nature and "have dominion" over it. The human species in the Judeo-Christian tradition, as we now see so clearly, "took that ball and ran with it." Yes, our creation stories have had a lot of power even until the present day. It would have been better, though, had we not chosen to ignore that part which declares *all* of the creation to be sacred in God's eyes.

It is almost amusing to contemplate the ridiculous arguments that have gone on and do go on about the creation story. There are those even in this last decade of century twenty who would argue the factual nature of the "Biblical story of creation" and even demand that it be taught in our schools. Which story? Shall we teach our children about the scientific evidence that the female of the species came from a rib of the male? Of course we have long been aware that such religious positions are more psychological than they are theological. Against such, rational arguments have no power. Needless to say, the creation stories of our tradition are all metaphorical in nature.

The problem with our creation stories now is not that they fail the test of scientific scrutiny. Many powerful and useful metaphors would fail that test. The problem is that those stories do not serve us well in this time of planetary crisis...do

---

[15] Joseph Campbell with Bill Moyers, Betty Sue Flowers, editor, *The Power of Myth* (New York, 1988), p. 56.

not "work" for us. They do not lead us into a relationship of mutuality with the rest of the creation. They are far too anthropocentric. Humans cannot anymore be considered as separate from the entirety of the creation. They will not survive as such. The actuality of it is that they are not separate. They are deeply inter-related with all of the universe and wholly dependent upon it for survival. In addition, our stories tell us of a God who is separate from the creation. This we now know to be a disastrous aspect of the stories. Many other creation stories tell of God being in the midst of the creation, in the trees, in the rocks, in the wind; but our stories speak of God as a separate entity in the creation. God is portrayed like a builder who builds a subdivision and walks away, leaving it in the hands of a "steward." Such a vision of God can be tolerated as long as the resources and resilience of the planet are seemingly without limit. Unfortunately, we no longer live in such a time. Shall we seek to salvage these stories? Are we not as capable of creating a story for our time as they were capable of doing in their time? Oh yes!

In these very days scientists and artists are about the task of telling the new creation story. This new creation story has several remarkable qualities. The first quality that we notice is that it is wondrous. This new story is filled with awe and wonder. As I have read it I have been staggered again and again by the incredible happening this universe is. Vast aeons of time and vast reaches of space and overwhelming cosmic events fill the screen of my mind. Imagine galaxies coming into being spontaneously across the universe, like snowflakes appearing on a wintry night. Imagine a tremor passing through the Milky Way galaxy and our sun coming into being. If one knows God as the Mystery of the universe, this new story will speak with power to her/him of the majesty of God.

The second quality of this new story is that it is "true." That doesn't mean that it is the final truth or that its teachings are absolute. We do not live in that kind of a universe. It is true in the sense that it is based solidly on the best knowledge available at this moment in time. Here is the good news for those who have been afraid of losing our ancient creation story under the onslaught of secularism: The new story is filled with the awareness of Mystery and the new story doesn't have to pretend about anything at all. Remember when we tried to argue that the earth was only six thousand years old in spite of dinosaur fossils which were verifiably one hundred and fifty million years old? Now we can put those tired old arguments to rest. The new creation story "does our God proud" and does it by embracing the truth as we know it. The old "creationism" war can be abandoned now. All of that energy can be put into seeing to it that the new creation story is told and told well across this planet.

The third quality of this new story is that it is universal. For the first time in history, the entire planet is learning this same story. All reputable schools and universities on this planet are teaching this story. It is the taken-for-granted story of the creation in all modern science classrooms. Religious leaders are still slow to embrace this story, but to the extent that they want their children to fully participate in the scientific and technological benefits of the next century, they must allow their children to learn this story. It is inseparable from the scientific revolution of our time. It is time now for us to examine our old creation stories and see whether they can be salvaged as metaphors. Do they tell the truth about the nature of God? Do they tell the truth about our actual situation on this little planet? If they pass these tests, they can still be told as metaphors. However, they will pale in comparison to the magnificence of our new story because the new story fits with what every school child is learning in school, and the new story is the same story that every other child on the planet will be learning. The power that this new story might have in bringing about a new and planetary sense of unity among us can, at this moment, only be imagined.

As I write these words, I am reading with fascination the book by Brian Swimme and Thomas Berry called *The Universe Story*. It begins with the primordial flaring forth some fifteen billion years ago. It moves on to the creation of the galaxies and the supernovas ten to fourteen billion years ago, the birth of the solar system five billion years ago, the creation of the earth four billion years ago, and then the pace picks up. We read the incredible story of the first living cell, the invention of photosynthesis, and the coming into being of the first multicellular animal. The story picks up details and drama as we relive the great ice ages, the formations of the continents, the vast extinctions and eventually the appearance of the first human. I cannot begin to do justice to our new story in this space, but I recommend *The Universe Story* as a wonderful way to get acquainted with it.

Swimme and Berry point out several themes of all existence. These themes are very important for us to understand. They will inform us concerning our relationship to the creation as it continues to unfold. The first theme is differentiation. This means that the universe will continue to change. It will not repeat itself. It will not operate in cycles. From the beginning the universe has been experimenting with the new. In our short experiences of time, we might view it as fixed and static. Such, we now know, has never been the case. "There has never been a time when the universe did not seek further differentiation."[16] Our own lives are a part of that experimentation with the novel and the unexpected. Our gift is that we get a chance to consciously and creatively participate in the movement of the universe toward the unknown. The seriousness of differentiation for our own time is that the earth's health is not locked into some static system as we have wanted to believe. The health of the earth is actually directly related to the decisions that we make.

The second governing theme in the universe is self-organization. Each thing in the universe...from galaxies to atoms...has the power to organize itself and relate itself to the entire cosmos. Molten rock had the capacity to bring forth, over a

---

[16] Brian Swimme and Thomas Berry, *The Universe Story* (San Francisco, 1992), p. 73.

period of time, living animals.[17] If rocks have that power, is it not possible that we human ones can find solutions to the problems which our civilization has created?

The third governing theme in the universe is communion. Other words which illuminate this theme are interrelatedness, interdependence, kinship, etc. "To be is to be related, for relationship is the essence of existence." "Alienation for a particle is a theoretical impossibility." "Each galaxy is directly connected to the hundred billion galaxies of the universe, and there will never come a time when a galaxy's destiny does not involve each of the galaxies in the universe."[18] When the universe is so thoroughly inter-dependent, how can it be that we have alienated ourselves from each other and from the natural world of which we are an inseparable part? It may be that this alienation is the very definition of the word "sin." Paul Tillich tried to teach us of the power of such separation. Now we see that our separation is an effort to deny the very nature of the cosmos itself. Can there be any healing for the blue planet short of our finding a way back to the truth? The new creation story is one way in which we are being invited to "come to ourselves" and return to our home. (Luke 15)

I dream of a day when Sunday School teachers who also teach in public schools will be able to share the wonder of the creation with their students in both schools. What a day it will be when the rather silly war between science and religion is a thing of the past. I dream of a day when the spirituality of the church (whatever "church" might be in such a day) will be fed directly by the wonder of the universe in which we live rather than by old and dry treatises from antiquity. God is being revealed in every facet of our universe and we are so blinded by our religion that we miss most of it. I dream of a new day. I dream of a day when our most important stories will "work" for us again.

---

[17] Ibid., p. 77.

[18] Ibid., p. 77.

CHAPTER SIX

PRACTICAL HELPS

Suppose a person wants to have a spirituality rooted in reality. How would such a person begin? Are there any guidelines? Certainly, this book has shown the danger inherent in creating rules and dogma regarding that which is mysterious. Nonetheless, it might be helpful to offer some broad directions from my own experience and from the experience of others who have sought to have their spirituality rooted in reality.

First, let's consider this question: What about church? Suppose a person is deeply involved in a local church or is considering becoming involved. Is that likely to be helpful? The answer is "maybe." I have been able to find a small group of people in several churches who were ready to work together on this task. Those groups were extremely helpful. It is even possible to find churches whose leadership is seeking a spirituality that is consistent with the realities of our present day, but such churches are still quite rare. One should be clear about the reality of the institutional church in our time. It is very heavily invested in the status quo, and has proven itself extremely resistant to significant change. Unless a person can find some like-minded folk there, it can prove to be a very lonely place to be. In addition, the heavy barrage of out-of-date imagery might be quite seductive at times. "What's wrong with me?" might be a frequent question in one's mind.

Some churches provide good fellowship and loving support. They may do many worthy things in the community. They probably support schools, hospitals and other worthy projects around the world. If you are deeply involved in such a church, your first step will be to search for like-minded people there. My experience is that when people get a fair introduction to a spirituality rooted in contemporary cosmology, they usually respond with enthusiasm. At the same time I should admit that I am pretty careful in selecting people to approach about this matter.

In any case, it will be very helpful to find "church" within which you can make your pilgrimage. By "church" I mean a community of people who have the same yearnings that you have for a new and relevant spirituality...a spirituality which enhances a sense of unity with the Mystery. A group of four to ten people can provide much support and can provide the depth of caring that many of us long for. It is difficult to persist in any difficult task unless we have some companions on the way.

My second suggestion is this: Get acquainted with the cosmos. Fall in love with the creation. Begin with the nearest flower or bird or spider web. Notice the wonder of the world around you. If you have a chance to watch one of your children being born, that is incomparable as a moment of awe. My earliest real break-through in this area was that moment in my youth when I saw the calf being born. The wonder of it still rattles my cage. Don't make the leap to abstraction that so often we are tempted to do. Don't begin to think, "There must be a God who created all of this." Let that thought go. Simply experience the wonder, and in so doing you are directly experiencing God. Get away from "ideas about God" and let yourself simply experience the Mystery in the midst of your life and of all creation.

My experience has been that I need my holy places. The seashore at sunrise is one. The Grand Canyon is another. The high Sierras in Yosemite are another place. Last summer a great place was in my den beside the window where I could see the profusion of wild flowers in my back yard. Make your pilgrimage to your holy places fairly often. The experience of the Holy is what you are after. Make that a high priority. It is also important to arrange for a good portion of solitary time at such a place. The experience of awe is much more likely where there is no chatter going on. I go backpacking and I have found it quite easy to find solitude...just walk further than five miles into the wilderness. Another sure-fire method is getting up early in the morning. In either case, the crowds thin out remarkably.

To further your acquaintance with the cosmos, I suggest reading books by people who are able to hear its music. *Pilgrim at Tinker Creek* by Annie Dillard is a wonderful beginning place. *The Immense Journey* by Loren Eisely is a classic in this area. Many other books could do just as well. Expand your reading in the area of science. Learn enough about astronomy to be amazed. Learn enough about sub-atomic physics to be amazed. Learn about the animals and birds and plants in your own back yard. Learn enough to be amazed at the Mystery. Learn enough about the new creation story to be blown away by the wonder of it. And don't forget your own body. What an incredible source of wonder its every function is. The fact that thoughts in my head translate so quickly to actions by my fingers on this keyboard is a miracle indeed. More mysterious are the thoughts themselves. What *are* they?

My third suggestion is this: Get freed up from the stories and dogma of the Christian faith. This suggestion assumes that you have been schooled in those matters. If you do not have that background, this suggestion will be of less value to you. For those of us who have been brought up in the church I believe this is a crucial suggestion. We must get free of the Christian story as "fact." There is no way we can treat factually stories that depend upon a world view that is not our own. We can translate those stories into our own world and make some sense of their message only if we are able to separate them from the vehicle of a past world view. As I have pointed out, it is symbol and story which speak to the soul. To put it differently, it is the "spirit" of the story that heals us, not the "letter" of the story. The "letter" tends to bind us.

In my own experience nothing is more helpful here than the series of tapes by Joseph Campbell with Bill Moyers. The book (noted in the bibliography) is an excellent second choice should the tapes not be available. These conversations with Joseph Campbell expand one's horizons. The role of mythology in the human adventure is revealed in its very broadest scope. Christian mythology is seen in that context. It can be a wonderfully freeing experience. It can set the stage for a grasp of the essential Christian message at a much deeper level. It also frees one up to see the weaknesses of the Christian tradition. At best, one gets a chance to make a whole new decision about the role of the Christian "religion" in his/her own spirituality.

My fourth suggestion is this: Read *Original Blessing* by Matthew Fox and get acquainted with Creation Spirituality. Especially will this be helpful for persons coming out of a strong Christian tradition. Creation Spirituality is the "other Christianity" that most of us have not had the privilege of knowing. It has historically been much more related to reality and has been (of course) much more related to the creation. There are many rich gifts in this tradition which have been very helpful to me.

Another advantage of studying the Creation Spirituality tradition is that it provides a structure for working on one's own spiritual journey. The four paths of this tradition seem to me to be on target for anyone seeking to grow spiritually. It is crucial to love the creation if we are to be "rooted in reality." It is crucial to be able to "let go and let be", if we are going to be able to be at peace with the passing-ness of all that is. It is crucial that we be able to acknowledge the creativity of the universe as it courses through our bodies if we are to be at one with the universe itself. And it is crucial that we experience our unity with all that is because that is simply the way it is. Without that sense of unity, our justice work will always be shallow with a tendency toward self-serving. I recommend the forms of Creation Spirituality even if a person rejects the Christian content of it. Actually, CS encourages a "deep ecumenism" that tends to break free of any traditional boundaries of religion.

It is worthy of special emphasis that our creativity must be set free. Certainly the church has de-emphasized human creativity for the past several centuries. We have all tended to be left-brain people. The third path of CS seeks to set our creativity free, but it is important that all of our spirituality be characterized by a full measure of right brain activity and emphasis. Draw pictures, paint pictures, write poems, make music, plant gardens, create new approaches to justice-making. When studying a book, be sure to make the study itself at least fifty percent right brain activity. Paint that chapter! Dance that chapter! Let the Milky Way's creative power reveal itself in your work. It is really true that the rational process is not our salvation. It has its gift to give, but the creative power of the universe cannot be contained by human rational thought. Our spirituality must acknowledge this truth.

Finally, our lives must change. The universe is on a journey. Every day is a new creation. Our lives when they get into close communion with the "way things are" will begin to change as well. It is a little test: What new is happening in my life? This is urgent for us in the context of American culture religion because we are so accustomed to religion that too easily embraces the status quo. It might be easy and even tempting for us to slip back into a kind of abstract spirituality which simply makes us feel good while being satiated with the accouterments of the good life. (Indeed it is this tendency in "New Age" spirituality which is its greatest weakness.) Every study session and every group meeting must have in it some conversation about the newness that is happening in me and how that relates to the needs of the larger creation. What is it that the Mystery is doing in me these days? Some mystic long ago suggested that God is forever young in that God is always new...is always being born among us. I believe that we can also be, in that sense, young until we die.

CONCLUSION

During these past months as I have worked on this book I have had a recurring experience. I would encounter some rather impressive event in the life of the church and I would wonder: "Can it be as bad as I say in my book?"

I attended a Tenebrae service on Good Friday. It was led by one of my dearest friends. The music was excellent. The readings were very well done. The mood was perfect. I was moved by the experience. Can this be so bad?

One of my colleagues told me about a recent funeral service for a victim of AIDS. He led the service. He allowed open witness to the victim's sexual orientation. It was obviously a very meaningful and comforting service for those who attended. Surely this is not so far removed from the real world.

A man is retiring in our United Methodist Conference this year. He is my hero. His capacity for selflessness and love is unsurpassed. Can a church which produced such a man be as far off base as I say?

Certainly I must give credit to the church for being of comfort to people in times of distress. Certainly I must give credit to the church for great music and art and for excellence in various programs of service. And certainly there has always been a "prophetic remnant" in the life of the church. Thank God for all of this. Surely I could not have survived these many years in ministry had these gifts not been present. The human adventure, however, deserves much more. The cosmos demands more. The crisis of our time requires more.

Can anyone argue that our religious stories and rituals and our very patterns of thought are really better when they are couched in the world-view of the first century? Is it not quite possible that when we "die" to the first century we might be resurrected in the twentieth century? I believe so. I have experienced that resurrection myself. We must articulate the gospel truth fearlessly in terms of the world in which we live.

Can anyone argue that our treatment of metaphor as fact has been helpful to us? The very power of a metaphor is that it is not fact. It speaks obliquely. It slides underneath one's consciousness. Make a fact out of it and it loses its power. It becomes an object among objects...like the price of eggs at the corner market. We must fearlessly declare our metaphors to be what they are. We must afford people the opportunity for a deeper grasp of the truth.

Can anyone argue that our separation from the cosmos has been helpful to us? How shallow and emaciated a faith becomes when it is separated from the Mystery that is hidden in every flower and in every child's laughter. How alienated must we be before our hearts will cry out for reunion? How far down the road to destruction must we go before our religion will let us see the essential unity of all creation?

And who can defend a religion which shamelessly hides in illusion? The heart of the Christian faith declares reality itself to be good and holy. All excuses for pretending are gone. There is no need to live in illusion when reality has been

83

declared trustworthy. Yes, the universe no longer has a second floor! Yes, our most central stories are metaphors! Yes, the Holy resides in the midst of the creation and is accessible to all! The people in the pews can stand reality. It will bless them. Reality is filled with holiness.

Try to imagine the following incident.

It was early in the morning and the pilots of squadron twenty-one had gathered in the briefing room. It was to be another day of routine training, but this morning was different. The squadron commander himself was there for the briefing. Something must be up. The training officer droned on through the normal material. This is the area for our exercises. This is the purpose. These are the dangers. Finally he finished and said, "Now Col. McKenzie has a few words to say." The Colonel stood up and said these words: "I am pretty worried about our training today. I was reading my Bible last night and I read that Jesus will be returning in the clouds very soon. It would be a great tragedy if one of our planes were to strike him. So I want you all to be especially careful. Keep your eyes peeled. And whatever you do, don't fly near any clouds."

Col. McKenzie was relieved of his duties. Without exception the pilots were convinced that he had lost his mental capacity to lead a squadron.

Many of the same pilots were in the base chapel on an earlier Sunday and the sermon was about the second coming of Christ. They heard the chaplain discuss the fact that someday soon Jesus was going to return and that according to the Bible he would come down from heaven in the clouds. They were not the least bit surprised and did not give the matter a second thought. When Col. McKenzie made his announcement, they did not even remember that the chaplain had discussed the same matter. The two worlds were thoroughly separate. A person would have to be a little bit insane to actually begin to look for Jesus among the clouds.

The pilots instinctively knew what this book is saying: The world view of "church" bears little resemblance to the world we live in and many of the central stories of that "church" world cannot be taken literally in this world.

It should come as no surprise that countless people now are searching for spirituality outside the confines of the Christian church and outside the confines of the other established religions. The world is filled with conflict and stress. Life can get to be pretty heavy and everyone needs a healthy way of relating to the actual world. Everyone senses that life is far more than what one sees with one's eyes, and there is a universal yearning for the capacity to "see through" to the deeps.

In addition, the planet as a whole is under attack. It is being destroyed by the species called human. The planet is crying out for the humans to find a healthy way of relating to the rest of creation. The planet is a little weary of the "blind guides" of religion leading the squadron off into unreal discussions about being careful around the clouds. Get real! Offer this troubled planet a spirituality that relates us joyfully and compassionately to the real.

And that, I suspect, is exactly what Jesus of Nazareth understood himself to be doing when he announced the Kingdom to be in our midst.

BIBLIOGRAPHY

Campbell, Joseph, with Bill Moyers, Betty Sue Flowers, ed. *The Power of Myth.* New York: Doubleday, 1988.

Capra, Fritjof. *The Tao of Physics.* New York: Bantam Books, 1984.

--- *The Turning Point.* New York: Bantam Books, 1983.

Dillard, Annie. *Pilgrim at Tinker Creek.* New York: Bantam Books, 1982.

Eiseley, Loren. *The Immense Journey.* New York: Vintage Books, 1957.

Fox, Matthew. *Original Blessing.* Santa Fe: Bear & Co., Inc. 1983.

--- *The Coming of the Cosmic Christ.* San Francisco: Harper and Row, 1988.

--- *WHEE! We, wee All the Way Home--* Santa Fe: Bear & Co., Inc. 1985.

Gebara, Ivone. "Ecofeminism and Panentheism." *Creation Spirituality.* November/December, 1993

Lawrence, D.H. *Selected Poems.* New York: The Viking Press, 1959.

Merton, Thomas. *Conjectures of a Guilty Bystander.* Garden City, N.Y.: Doubleday and Company, Inc., 1966.

--- *Contemplation in a World of Action.* Garden City, N.Y.: Doubleday and Company, Inc., 1971.

O'Conner, Flannery. *The Complete Stories.* New York: The Noonday Press, 1992.

Robinson, John A.T. *Honest to God.* Philadelphia: Westminister Press, 1963.

Schilpp, P.A., ed. *Albert Einstein: Philosopher-Scientist.* Peru (IL): Open Court, 1970.

Swimme, Brian, and Thomas Berry. *The Universe Story.* San Francisco: Harper Collins, 1992.

Walker, Alice. *The Color Purple.* New York: Washington Square Press, 1982.